# TEEN LEADERSHIP REVOLUTION

*How Ordinary Teens Become Extraordinary Leaders*

## TOM THELEN

FOR EVERY TEEN WHO WANTS TO
SERVE A GREATER PURPOSE
AND LIVE A BETTER STORY.

# TABLE OF CONTENTS

|  |  | INTRODUCTION | i |
|---|---|---|---|
| Chapter 1 | A Character Intervention | 01 |
| Chapter 2 | Bullyproof | 11 |
| Chapter 3 | Pain Into Purpose | 29 |
| Chapter 4 | Four Types of People | 39 |
| Chapter 5 | Four Levels of Leadership | 51 |
| Chapter 6 | Self-Discipline | 61 |
| Chapter 7 | Responsibility | 71 |
| Chapter 8 | Respect | 79 |
| Chapter 9 | Honesty | 87 |
| Chapter 10 | Fairness | 97 |
| Chapter 11 | Citizenship | 105 |
| Chapter 12 | A Bigger Story | 111 |
| Chapter 13 | A Unified Team | 119 |
| Chapter 14 | Secrets to Success | 131 |
| Appendix I | Make it Happen | 136 |
| Appendix II | TLR MANIFESTO | 137 |

# INTRODUCTION

Hey you! Yes, you... sitting there reading this book with one hand, and playing Fruit Ninja with the other. I'm talking to you because, well... I was you. I was an ordinary teen. Nothing about me stood out as spectacular or awesome. I wasn't the captain of the football team, or the braniac, or the prom king. I was just a face in the crowd.

At least that's how this all started.

So if you feel average, there is hope. The good news is great leaders are not born as great leaders. Nope. They start out as Simple Suzy and Jack McNormal, just like you and me. They experience pain, heartache, victory, and defeat. And just like you and me, they have to discover how to turn their pain around for a positive purpose. This principle is what separates average teens from awesome leaders who go the distance, and it's exactly what this book is all about: how to turn your pain into a purpose and how to become a great leader along the way.

We all know teens who turn 18, move out of the house, and go off the deep end with their newfound freedom. We see them fall into toxic choices, and we watch as their lives spin out of control. It's a common story. So why is it that some students fall apart after high school, while others go on to become great leaders?

I believe that successful students follow an unwritten code of character, leadership, and relationships – standards that guide their life through the highest highs and lowest lows. These teens are grounded in positive character, committed to sound leadership principles, and devoted to healthy relationships. This book contains concrete principles that can be the guard rails of your life, holding you on course when the path gets slippery and propelling you to new levels of success when the climb gets steep.

These principles have been around for centuries in every culture of the world. Iconic leaders from Jesus to Gandhi, to Martin Luther King Jr. have taught these universal values and lived them out as examples for the rest of us. But it starts with the choices of one teen – and that's you. This book is about the real life choices and actions of teens who want to turn their pain into a gain and achieve a purpose worth living for. Teens just like you.

○ ○ ○

Think of this book as more of a compass than a map[1]. Maps show you the exact route from here to there. Maps are great when you know exactly where you are and exactly where you want to go. But in life, we all start in different places, and we want to end up in different places. You may not even know where we are right now, much less where you want to go. So the exact route that each of us must take is going to be different, and creating a successful map for one person can lead another person

---

[1] "The Map Has Been Replaced by the Compass." Seth Godin's Blog. N.p., 21 Feb. 2012. <http://sethgodin.typepad.com/

way off course. Each of us has a different route to becoming the best version of ourselves.

The compass is great because it always points north no matter what. Come rain or shine, the compass is always there to guide you. You can be completely lost, and the compass still points north. Let these principles guide you to the true north in your life. It's the only way to become the person you were meant to be.

As you read the chapters, think about how the principles apply to your life. What does it mean in the real world where you live? At the end of each chapter, I've included a study guide. This is a tool for you (or your group of friends) to implement the principles on a more personal level. Reading about the principles is only a start. It's not until you act on them that you are able to change yourself and the world around you.

As we jump into the foundations of leadership, we will discover that it's all about who you are on the inside that shapes who you are on the outside. We will find the secrets of success are not about being the loudest, the smartest, the tallest, or the richest. The real building blocks of leadership are stacked one at a time, in the ordinary lives of ordinary teens. Teens just like you.

This is how the **TEEN LEADERSHIP REVOLUTION** begins.

# CHAPTER ONE

# A CHARACTER INTERVENTION

When I was 15 I made a discovery that changed my life forever. It was the realization that character determines my destiny. Leading up to sophomore year in high school, I had developed a victim mentality. Life had dealt me a bad hand. I was short for my age, I had allergies and asthma, my dad hated me (I thought), my teachers wanted me to fail, and on and on. The truth was, there were a lot of things I didn't like about myself. And since there were so many things I didn't like about myself, I decided to do the most logical thing and just... be somebody else.

So I became Funny Tom. I was like, "WhaHoo! Look at me everyone! ...insert funny joke here..." Funny Tom made everyone laugh, which felt really good. Funny Tom was the life of the party, which felt really important. Pushing the envelope of acceptable behavior was my new drug of choice. It was addicting. I would do anything to get a laugh: make fun of myself, make fun of my friends, my teachers, you name it.

There was a time when I toilet papered a house with over 100 rolls of toilet paper. At that point it feels like less of a prank and more of a financial investment. I was into toilet paper like bankers were into stocks and bonds.

My life was on a slippery slope. And at the time, I didn't even know it. At the age of 15, I wasn't thinking about slippery slopes. I had my class-clown image to maintain. That was my new fulltime job, and I enjoyed it. But the tough part about trying so hard to be someone else is that it becomes very difficult to be...

yourself.

Because you're busy being someone else.

Who cares! I was busy being Funny Tom, and it felt good, dag nabbit.

But not everyone was laughing. In my acting out, I was starting to miss assignments at school. I was mouthing off to all the wrong people at all the wrong times. At home, the conflict between my parents and I was getting worse every day, and they were threatening to kick me out of the house. It was obvious to everyone except me – the wheels of my life were starting to fall off.

Then I was called to a "special meeting" at my school. The meeting itself didn't make me feel very special at all, but what followed the meeting would change my life forever.

So there I was, sitting in the classroom with all my teachers, the principal, my parents, and me.

Just me.

Surrounded by people, but completely alone.

I wanted to melt through the floor, or better yet, strap on some jet pack and shoot out the window, saluting the crowd with my middle finger. *Take that, suckers!*

None of that happened. Instead, I was put on academic probation, which is a fancy way of saying *"One more thing, and you're out of here mister!"*

After the meeting, my English Teacher, Mrs. Burdick, asked if she could talk with me and my parents. We agreed. Mrs. Burdick told us about a counseling program that she and Mr. Burdick offered on their farm. It was a three-week program for young men who needed a "character intervention," whatever that meant. The Burdicks had been in education and farming for many years, and now as young grandparents, they offered a counseling program for young men.

Mrs. Burdick said it was too-late for many boys my age since the "concrete of life was already setting up." But then she said she believed I could still change – if I wanted to. And right then and there she asked if I wanted to come to the counseling program.

Three weeks.

On a farm.

In counseling.

My head was spinning. I was thinking,

> *I don't wanna go! All my friends will find out. Everyone will know that I'm a failure. I'll never get a girlfriend. No one will like me. They'll think I'm a freak! THERE IS NO WAY I'M GOING TO DO THIS!*

But through my tears and insecurities, I heard my own voice say, "Yeah, I'll go." And then I said to myself, *"Shut up Voice! Who asked you anyway?!!"*

I really came that close to saying no. I mean I almost gave in to my fears and insecurities. Then I realized something: Mrs. Burdick was *for me*, not against me. She wanted me to succeed and was willing to invest in me. She believed in me, even if I didn't believe in myself. The whole time my brain was shouting at me, telling me not to go, but my heart was saying something different. My heart said go.

Sometimes the hardest decisions in life are also the best decisions you ever make.

So I went.

Life on the Burdick Farm was tough. I had to wake up each morning at 5am to do the farm chores before school. Then, even after a full day of school, I was in charge of making supper every night. Very tolerant people, the Burdicks, or maybe they just had low standards for food. My meals were pretty terrible, but they didn't complain.

And after supper they would counsel me. I remember them saying "Tom, you are not a victim... you always have the ability to respond." And Mrs. Burdick would always say, *"Tom, your response is your responsibility."* (It had a nice ring to it.)

They kept driving home their point that *character determines your destiny*. I would just sit there not knowing what to say.

Mrs. Burdick would ask, "Tom, how are you feeling right now?" And I'd respond "I dunno." Then she'd say, "How are you feeling in your heart?" And I'd be like, "I dunno! What is this, Doctor Phil? I don't know!!!"

I didn't know it at the time, but I was using sarcasm to cover up the hurts beneath the surface of my life. I was laughing on the outside, and dying on the inside. And that was when the Burdicks wrote these words out on a piece of paper:

**FEEL - THINK - SAY - DO - HABIT - CHARACTER**

They said,

> Tom, how you feel matters, because that's the
> beginning of the character process. It starts with how
> you **feel**. It moves to what you **think**. What you think
> becomes what you **say**. What you say turns into what
> you **do**. If you do it long enough it becomes a **habit**...
> and those habits form your **character**.

I never thought about it that way before, but they were
right. They're still right. The process is still true today. But
let me give you the surprising truth I learned along the
way. The real power of the character development
process is not in the terms themselves; it is in *the dash
between the terms* that really matters. The *choice*
between every action – that's what changes everything.

You might not be able to control how you **feel**, but you
can *choose* what you **think** about. And when you think
about it, you have a *choice* of what you **say** *(and what you
choose not to say)*. From there, you *choose* what you **do**.
You then have a *choice* of what you do over and over
again, and those actions turn into **habits**. And the habits
you *choose* become the **character** of your life.

This process of character development can essentially be
boiled down to the dash between each step of the
process – the choices you make.

I'm talking about choices like who influences you, what
music you listen to, what you watch online, who you hang
out with, how you handle pain, who you choose to

forgive, and the list goes on. You are surrounded by choices every minute of every day. Will you read the next paragraph or run around the room with a towel over your head? Hey, it's your choice.

And if you really desire to make the right choices – the choices that are going to help turn you into the best version of yourself – then you must commit to making the tough decisions that lead to long term success.

What we're talking about is self-discipline, a subject we'll address later on.

In the chapters that follow, we'll take a more in-depth look at specific principles that will develop you as a leader. Nobody said this journey would be easy. But know this: nothing of great value comes without great sacrifice.

# CHAPTER ONE STUDY GUIDE

1. One a scale of one to ten with ten being the best, how would you rate the strength of your character?

2. Have to ever tried to "be somebody else" at your school? Why do you think so many teens have a hard time being themselves?

3. What are some of the most common pressures teens are facing at your school?

4. In this chapter I described how the "wheels of my life" were falling off. When was the last time you felt like your life was falling apart? What led you there?

5. What is your greatest strength and biggest weakness in the character process of: *feeling, thinking, saying, doing, habits, and character?*

6. What is one positive step you can do today to strengthen your character? Write out one action step in the space below and commit to making it happen.

# CHAPTER TWO

# BULLYPROOF

I gasped for breath as the bully pulled my head out of the water for a brief second, only to slam me back beneath the cold waves of Gull Lake. I was thirteen and at summer camp. I'll never forget that day. How many times does somebody have to hold your head under water to completely break your will power? I would say about six times. Yes, six times will do it. I remember choking out swear words at the bully in between submersions, but I eventually gave up. There was nothing I could do physically, verbally, or emotionally to stop him. I felt like such a loser. A small crowd gathered but no one stood up for me, and no one talked about it afterward.

Neither did I. I wanted that event erased from history.

Almost all of us have experienced moments like this where we were at the complete mercy of a bully. 90% of students between the 4th and 8th grade report being victims of bullying[2]. Nine out of ten students – that's pretty much all of us, and for many kids, the bullying starts at an early age.

The other night we went to Chuck E. Cheese (or as I like to call it, *The Kiddie Casino*) with our four kids: Addie - age 5, Jack - age 3, and our twins Ellie and Lucy - age 1. Toward the end of the night we told Addie she had five minutes left to play. She bounded off with freedom while Casie and I kept a closer eye on the younger three. The five minutes came and went, and we started to look for Addie. She was nowhere to be found. Panic started to set in, and we began to fear the worse. Just when we were about to contact the restaurant staff, I spotted Addie way up high inside the giant play structure... cornered and crying at the dead end of a tunnel. I hollered at her to come down, and eventually she arrived at the bottom of the slide, soaked in her own tears.

> *What's wrong honey? Are you okay?*

> *I couldn't come down because of the bullies.* (She says, sobbing into my shirt.)

> *What do you mean, honey? What happened?*

---

[2] "Bullying Statistics 2010." BullyingStatistics.Org, n.d. Web. 18 Feb. 2012.
<http://www.bullyingstatistics.org/content/bullying-statistics-2010.html>.

*The bullies wouldn't let me come down. They called me stupid and said I was a little poop head, so I had to stay up there. Now I'm never gonna go back.*

She went on to describe the whole story and how she hadn't provoked them and hadn't fought back – the only thing she could do was run away. We explained how proud we were of her for not fighting back, but even with our encouragement she still cried most of the way home. Since then we've had some frank discussions about how to recognize and respond to bullying.

Calling someone a stupid poop-head might not seem like much to you, but put yourself in the shoes a five year old little girl. Two boys twice your size give you your first verbal beat down, just for the satisfaction of it. Meanwhile you're all alone with no one to rescue you.

It was traumatizing. Addie met her first bullies.

Stories like these are more common than you might think, and for a lot of students, it only gets worse from here.


## HI, MY NAME IS BOB

I recently spoke at a conference for the National Association of Student Councils, and after my first speech I met a student named Pat (I've omitted his real name for the sake of privacy). Pat was a bright young guy, about 16, who had just been voted to the National Board of

Directors for the conference. Quite an accomplishment for such a young teen. He explained to me how he had attended a private school for most of his life, but after years of relentless bullying and after a verbal lashing from a teacher (in front of his whole class), his parents let him drop out and switch to a public school. The new school was a chance to start over, and that is exactly what Pat did. But this time things would be different. His whole life he had been picked on and bullied for his name, but at the new school no one had to know his real name. So during the first six months he told everyone his name was Bob. Out of all the names he could have picked, he chose Bob. He didn't go with anything exotic, like Fabian, or Marc-Anthony. Nope… just Bob.

Pat was willing to give up his own identity to avoid the bullying and ridicule that had followed him since grade school. He was willing to become a completely different person. This was a reasonable choice to him.

When the truth eventually came out, he was devastated, and he found himself, once again, starting all over trying to win new friends.

○ ○ ○

How far are you willing to run from your bullies? To another room? To another school? Another life? If you feel alone or depressed, it's time to get help. It's time to talk with a trusted adult. Harming the bully or harming yourself is never the solution. There is a better way.

# THE CURRENT SYSTEM

In the 1970s, a psychology professor named Dr. Dan Olweus began surveying schools to get accurate data on bullying[3]. Since that time, the subject has grown into a whole field of study with mountains of evidence for schools to sift through. Over the years, the research has done a great job of identifying *the extent* of the problem, but it has done a poor job of finding solutions that actually work to reduce bullying. In over 30 years of anti-bullying research and prevention programs, the problem of bullying still taunts us, and new studies show it is actually getting worse[4]. But why?

Most bullying prevention programs assume the victimization of students, so they focus on teaching kids how to get help. Students are taught to anticipate being bullied and to report every incident. The message is:

## VICTIMS + HELP + BOUNDARIES = PREVENTION

The traditional goal is to end all bullying and create bully-free schools. This is a noble concept, so why hasn't it worked? Where are all the bully-free schools? We've had 30-plus years of research and 30-plus years of solutions. Where are the success stories?

---

[3] "A Brief History of the Olweus Bullying Prevention Program." Violence Prevention Works. Hazelden, n.d. Web. 21 Nov. 2011. <http://www.violencepreventionworks.org/public/o

[4] "Student Reports of Bullying and Cyber-Bullying." National Center for Education Statistics. U.S. Department of Education, 1 May 2011. Web. 13 Apr. 2012. <nces.ed.gov/pubs2011/2011316.pdf>.

Answer: There aren't any. 100% bully-free schools, that is.

They don't exist.

The truth is: the problem of bullying isn't going away. It is something that all of us have to face throughout life. Even if you *could* create a bully-free school, it would not prepare you to face the real world after high school where there is no virtual-police to swoop in and save you from the mean looks of your coworkers or to rescue you from the hurtful comments on facebook.

Despite the best intentions, anti-bullying programs often create a culture of victims. The bullied student becomes a victim of the bullying, and the bully becomes a victim of the system itself. So instead of preventing bullying, kids merely learn how to keep score.

The religious leader Mahatma Gandhi said, *"An eye for an eye only ends up making the whole world blind.[5]"* It's true: when we learn to keep score, everyone becomes a victim.

Please don't misunderstand. I am not suggesting we go back to the old school policies of *"sticks and stones may break my bones…,"* or *"Kids will be kids."* We cannot simply leave students to fend for themselves. We need the prevention programs and policies, but if we do what we've always done, we will *get what we've always got.*

---

[5] "Mahatma Gandhi Quotes - BrainyQuote." Famous Quotes at BrainyQuote. N.p., n.d. Web. 21 Aug. 2012. <http://www.brainyquote.com/quotes/

To make significant progress with our bullying prevention programs, we must change our focus. We must learn how to turn *victims* into *victors*.

# BULLYING BASICS

The U.S. Government recently launched a new website called StopBullying.Gov. On it, they define bullying as *"unwanted, aggressive behavior among school aged children that involves a real or perceived power imbalance."* In other words, bullying can be boiled down to one key ingredient: **the unwanted taking of power**. We see this in the animal kingdom when the "alpha" (the biggest, most aggressive animal) assumes control over the herd, physically dominating the other animals to bring them under his control. But we are not animals. We live in a civil society where all people are created equal. Short and tall, black and white – we all have equal value. In schools, this *taking of power* happens in four main ways:

1. **PHYSICAL BULLYING**: Hitting, pushing, spitting, violence, taking someone's things.

2. **VERBAL BULLYING**: Name calling, sexual harassment, teasing, taunting.

3. **SOCIAL BULLYING**: Excluding someone on purpose, publically embarrassing, or berating.

4. **CYBERBULLYING**: online harassment, sharing inappropriate photos, mean texts or posts.

We've researched it, labeled it, and tried to solve it, yet the bullying still continues on every campus across the globe. We cannot escape the truth that the current system of bullying prevention is broken in most schools. So what can be done?

# A NEW (OLD) METHOD

Instead of asking, *"How can we eliminate bullying?,"* we need to start asking, *"How can we turn victims into victors? How can we develop resilient students who can withstand the storms of life and respond appropriately to bullying and conflict?"*

The answer is surprisingly simple, and yet incredibly profound. It's called: **The Golden Rule**, which traditionally states *"Do unto others as you would have them do unto you.[6]"* In other words: *treat everyone the way you want to be treated – especially your enemies.* As easy as this sounds, it is actually very difficult to apply because it goes against the animal instinct to defend and fight back. The beauty is: when you love your enemies it empowers you, and it removes the power of the bullying. They go out of control, and you stay in control.

This universal principle has been taught through the ages by iconic leaders from Confucius to Buddha to Jesus who said in Luke 6:27, *"Love your enemies, do good to those*

---

[6] World Scripture - The Golden Rule ." Unification. N.p., n.d. Web. 2 Dec. 2010. <http://www.unification.net/ws/theme015.htm>.

*who hate you."* In today's world of common sense, The Golden Rule gives us much needed uncommon sense.

Now, it is important to note that this principle was never intended merely for your friends. Everyone likes people who like them back. It was written as an instruction for how to deal with difficult people: how to deal with bullies. The Golden Rule is an incredibly refreshing concept. Instead of keeping score, the new solution becomes:

### LOVE + BOUNDARIES + HELP = VICTORS

Learning this strategy will empower you and literally change your future. YOU CAN respond to bullies without fighting back or running away! YOU CAN live life as a *victim* or as a *victor* – it's your choice.

## SOLUTION 1 – LOVE YOUR BULLIES

- **BE A FRIEND:** Practice The Golden Rule and treat everyone as friends... especially your enemies. This is often called the Law of Reciprocity, meaning, *you get what you give.* Give love, and you receive it in return.

- **MAKE A FRIEND:** Realize that bullies are hurting people who need friendship, acceptance, and forgiveness. So turn your enemy into a friend.

- **RESOLVE CONFLICT:** Sometimes bullies will be reasonable if you talk with them after the fact in a safe place. Ask them to help you find a solution.

- **CREATE CULTURE:** Set the social tone for your school. Be the change, so bullying is viewed as abnormal.

## SOLUTION 2 – SET BOUNDARIES

- **DIFFUSE:** Bullies are looking for a reaction, so don't give them one! Being defensive only adds fuel to the fire, so take time to think before responding.

- **DON'T CARRY IT:** Remember when you fail to forgive, you become a prisoner of your own bitterness; you end up doing time for someone else's crime!

- **LAUGH IT OFF:** We all make mistakes, so when you do, be confident enough to laugh at yourself.

- **CHANGE THE DEFINITION:** Don't try to live up to someone else's definition of what is cool. Change the definition to accept yourself for *who you already are.*

## SOLUTION 3 – BE THE HELP

- **BE THE HELP:** You have the power to speak up whenever you see bullying happen. More than half of the time when you do, the bullying stops within 10 seconds[7]. So be brave and speak up for the silent!

---

[7] "BRAVE - Bullying Resources and Values Education." Family Resources Facilitation Program. N.p., n.d. Web. 18 Aug. 2012. <http://www.frfp.ca/BRAVE/bullying_stats.htm>.

- **GET SOME HELP:** Telling is not tattling. When a situation is serious, sexual, or repeated, tell an adult. Asking for help is actually a sign of strength, not weakness. Hiding your pain only leads to isolation.

Together, these solutions can create a new culture at your school, but they will only work if **you** take action. You may have been hurt. You may have been the victim, and that's real. But it is your choice to get bitter or to get better.

○ ○ ○

One of the nasty side effects of bullying is that sometimes the bullied-kid becomes the bully. By late middle school, this was the case for me. I was tired of being called short, being excluded from social groups, and generally being pushed around. I let the bullies get to me, and I became a very bitter person. Overtime, I found myself using sarcasm to lift myself up while putting other people down. I was being a bully, and I didn't even realize it. And without the intervention and love of one teacher, my life would have continued down that path.

Here's the thing: most bullies don't even realize the hurt they're causing themselves and others... and they will never know until someone stands up and says something.

All kids witness bullying. It will happen around you before you even realize it, and you will find yourself being a bystander. The important thing to remember is to decide ahead of time how you will respond. Will you just sit there in silence, providing an audience for the bully, becoming a silent supporter? Or will you face your fears, speak up for the silent, and create a new culture at your school?

○ ○ ○

As you read this, you might realize that - at times - you have been the bully. You and your friends have been the ones to cause the hurt. You intentionally excluded someone from your group, or you made fun of someone for the way they looked. But today is a new day. Right now is the time to go seek forgiveness, so put the book down and go do the right thing. For real.

Now is the time to be the change.

# 10 SOLUTIONS FOR SCHOOLS

As a youth speaker, I have the privilege of helping schools develop bullying prevention programs that create cultures of character in students, families, and communities. In the United States we have an uphill climb compared to many European countries that require classes on ethics in K-12 schools. We use character education programs to supplement our traditional classes. The good news is: we can learn from the best practices and the research to discover what really works. The next two pages contain 10 SOLUTIONS FOR SCHOOLS seeking to prevent bullying and empower students:

1. **VICTIMS TO VICTORS:** Teach students that bullying prevention starts with them. Show them how to resolve conflict and how to stand up for each other. Put the primary focus on empowering the bullied student and giving a voice to the bystanders.

2. **PARTNER WITH PARENTS:** Create a close connection between the families and the school. Provide chances for parents to share your mission of character growth. Ask parents to come to the school for more everyday events like lunch time and recess.

3. **MATCH WITH MENTORS:** Programs are helpful, but nothing empowers a student more than one-on-one mentorship. Kids Hope USA works with churches to provide volunteer mentors that meet with students at the school for one hour, once a week. Google it!

4. **REAL RESOURCES:** Purchase some good books and videos on self-esteem, character, and teen leadership, and give them to students when they need help. Host special events and quality school assemblies to create defining moments in the lives of your students.

5. **PRAISE THE POSITIVE:** Psychology has proven that it takes FIVE positive comments to overcome ONE negative comment[8]. Repeatedly praise your students for their good choices... and then do it again.

---

[8] Baumeister, Roy, Ellen Bratslavsky, Catrin Finkenauer, and Kathleen Vohs. "Bad Is Stronger Than Good." Review of General Psychology 5.4 (2001): 323-370. Print.

6.   **BYE-BYE BYSTANDERS:** 85% of bullying incidents involve bystanders, yet they only intervene 10% of the time[9]! However, when students do intervene, the bullying usually stops within 10 seconds[7]. Remind your students how important it is to speak up!

7.   **CHOOSE SOME CHAMPIONS:** Hand pick some students, staff, and parents to champion the cause of bullying prevention in your school. Have them plan a school assembly or an anti-bullying week. Let them research and select some follow-up curriculum.

8.   **BETTER BOUNDARIES:** With today's technology, teens are more connected than ever, which means much of the bullying can fly beneath the radar. Expand your anti-bullying program to include guidelines and training sessions on cyberbullying.

9.   **TEACHER TRAINING:** After the students, teachers are typically the next to respond to bullying. Have the school counselor(s) plan an in-service training session on bullying prevention and classroom management.

10. **CULTURE OF CHARACTER:** When bullies are expected, victims are collected. So set the opposite expectation: a culture of character where students learn to live out The Golden Rule. Slowly change the social climate of the school so bullying is viewed as abnormal.

---

[9] Jeffrey, Linda R., Ph.D.The Prevention Researcher, Volume 11, Number 3, 2004, Pages 7-8, and Item. "The Prevention Researcher." The Prevention Researcher. N.p., n.d. Web. 18 Aug. 2012. < http://www.tpronline.org/article.cfm/Bullying_Bystanders >.

These solutions work in symphony when people of character rise up and decide to live differently. Relying solely on an external solution to an internal heart problem will do nothing more than continue the culture of victimization.

We must empower our bullying prevention programs with the virtue of love and the wisdom of The Golden Rule if we ever want to create a culture of character in our schools. This is our shared mission.

It truly is a new (old) way.

# CHAPTER TWO STUDY GUIDE

1. When was the first (or last) time a bully got the best of you? How did you respond?

2. Is there a "victim culture" at your school? What can you do to change the culture of your school?

3. How does The Golden Rule empower students and remove power from bullies?

4. Of the SOLUTIONS FOR STUDENTS, which ones are you currently doing well, and where do you need the most improvement?

5. If you could convince your friends to do one thing about bullying at your school, what would it be?

6. Write the name of one specific bully you need to forgive. How can you practice The Golden Rule to change this relationship?

# CHAPTER THREE

# PAIN INTO PURPOSE

My wife Casie was held-back in first grade for spending too much time talking and drawing in class. She enjoyed school, and she was kind to everyone, but because she was not able to stay on task like the other kids, she was granted another round of first grade.

Case was, and still is... an artist. Artists don't thrive very well in push-down, assembly-line education models. They're much more hands-on. They need to interact and taste life with all of their senses. I could go on and on about different "philosophies of education" and how the system has improved over the years, but that's not the point of this chapter. The point is: Casie was hurt. She was devastated.

Again, I'm not pointing the finger or making her a victim, I'm simply stating the obvious – that kids who are held back in school are burdened with a tremendous load of mental and emotional baggage. That baggage often turns to guilt, shame, and insecurity, and over time it comes to define the person. The sad thing is: a lot of teens go through life without ever recognizing their deepest wounds, much less, healing from them.

I didn't meet Casie until a decade later in high school. We met at a local youth group where she played guitar in the band. I had recently started playing guitar, so it was a natural connection. Plus I thought she was hot, so that was a good motivator... but I digress.

Over the years we became best friends, but we didn't officially date until after high school (which is a great story that I'll save for another time). And in our early twenties, we married.

During that first year of marriage I remember being increasingly aware of how often Casie would make fun of herself. If she made a mistake or if she said the wrong thing, she would jokingly remark that she was dumb. Sometimes she would even say things like, *"Oh my word, I'm so stupid."* Now keep in mind, my wife is the most kindhearted person I know. Her greatest strength is building people up. She would never call anyone else dumb or stupid, not even as a joke.

When you're married, you become "one" with the other person, so when they hurt, you hurt too. I found myself not understanding my wife's sarcasm toward herself, and over time it even began to hurt my heart. I felt like she was holding herself back — like her jokes were affecting her own view of how far she could go in life. Her self-efficacy, as the scholars call it. I started remarking back that she's not stupid and she should stop saying things like that.

She agreed, but she didn't stop.

I got more serious about it, and in the months to follow we talked deeper and deeper about her past. She knew she wasn't stupid, but she sure joked about it a lot. By this time in our lives, my wife had become a successful hair stylist. She was a great wife, a wonderful friend, and a volunteer in the community. Everyone just loved her. There was nothing in my wife that would have pointed to her being a victim of her past hurts.

Nothing except... her treatment of herself. These jokes. These jokes that felt like tiny knives.

One day I put my foot down. *"Stop it honey! You cannot call my wife that. I know you're joking, but seriously, you have to stop saying that stuff about yourself. It hurts me, and I think it's hurting you more than you even realize."*

As much as she agreed, stopping was almost impossible because it had become second nature for her — she didn't even realize she was doing it. For at least the next year I kept sticking up for her... to herself. *"Don't call my wife that!"* I would not give up. No one was allowed to call my wife dumb or stupid, not ever herself.

○ ○ ○

Einstein once said, *"Everybody is a genius. But if you judge a fish by its ability to climb a tree, it will live its whole life believing that it is stupid.*[10]*"*

Maybe in your pain, you've begun to believe the lie. Uncovering the pain of your past is one of the most difficult things you will ever do. A lot of people burry the hurt so deep that they never go back to revisit it. It's simply too painful.

Over time, many of us accept the labels that are placed on us by society, by our pasts, by our hurts. Casie wasn't the first person to call herself dumb. That wound had been inflicted by bullies at her school, by teachers who didn't understand her learning style, even by family and friends. And because she had never dealt with the pain, she ultimately accepted the lie and lived with the label.

To protect herself from more hurt, she had learned to make fun of herself. It's hard for other people to call you dumb when you beat them to it. And we all have defense mechanisms like this – things we do to protect ourselves from more pain. Think of the girl who was sexually abused

---

[10] "Albert Einstein Quotes." Good Reads. N.p., n.d. Web. 7 June 2012.
<http://www.goodreads.com/author/quotes/9810

and never learns to give real hugs, or the guy who was cut from the team and decides to never play sports again, or the kid who was bullied and then becomes the bully.

It's just true: hurt people, hurt people.

In our hurts, we learn to live with hidden boundaries. We become limited by the invisible expectations of our pasts. As victims, our anger turns outward. *You did this to me. If you wouldn't have done this, I wouldn't have done that. It's your fault. If you only knew what it's like to be me!*

Healthy people have the opposite attitude. It's the attitude of I. *I can do this. I am responsible for my actions. I am the person who determines how far I can go in life. I may have been hurt in my past, but I am healing from that.* It's the attitude of personal responsibility.

○ ○ ○

I found freedom through the Burdick's farm and their intervention in my life. And on the other side of my pain is where I found the greatest purpose for my life. Now my mission is to help other people find that same freedom.

What matters is not who hurt you or how you were hurt; what matters is how you heal from that pain and how you turn that pain into a purpose.

Casie has done the same thing. Today, as the owner of her own hair salon, she teaches her employees how to empower other women. Who better to help a woman with pain and insecurity, than another woman who is being freed from her own pain and insecurity?

And you have the same opportunity before you. I don't know what baggage you're carrying or who gave it to you, but I know this: if you can accept the freedom of forgiveness, you can discover the purpose for your future. And the greatest purpose of your life is often right on the other side of your pain.

## IT'S JUST TRUE:
## FREE PEOPLE, FREE PEOPLE

Recently Casie and I were swapping embarrassing stories and she told about her first day in middle school. When the first bell rang, she accidentally ended up in the wrong classroom... surrounded by kids one year ahead of her, many of whom had been her first grade classmates. When the teacher told her she was in the wrong classroom, she was mortified. She left the room completely humiliated, as the other kids made comments that cut like knives. Sometimes Case still has nightmares where she relives that embarrassing moment. It followed her for decades. And when the memories come back, she forgives again.

You forgive again, so you can live again.

You may find freedom in forgiveness, just as I have, just as Casie did, but you need to remember that forgiveness comes in waves.

You forgive as completely as you can. You give it everything you have, and you find freedom. But then the bitterness tries to creep back in. You discover an old memory and it's like opening a scar and feeling the wound all over again. What do you do?

You forgive again. And with that forgiveness, you get the gift of being free – free to be fully you. Free to turn your pain into a purpose.

# CHAPTER THREE STUDY GUIDE

1. Why do you think it was so hard for Casie to stop making fun of herself?

2. Take a minute to think back over your life. What have been some of the deepest hurts and pains you've experienced along the way?

3. Circle the experience that has had the most negative effect on you.

4. Have you ever felt limited by the pain or mistakes of your past? Why or why not?

5. Who do you need to forgive the most in your life? Why?

6. What would it look like for you to forgive the people or past events that hurt you the most? (Even if that means keeping your distance from unhealthy people).

# CHAPTER FOUR

# FOUR TYPES OF PEOPLE

Fifty years ago a small group of young people decided to do something that would move them from ordinary to extraordinary. They decided to step up and stand out for what they believed in – the principle that all people should be treated and valued equally, a principle known as civil rights.

These young people would come to be known as The Freedom Riders[11], but at the moment, they were just ordinary young people and college students. They were normal kids who went to class each day, did their homework each night, and dreamed that one day their lives would mean something.

---

[11] Freedom Riders. Dir. Stanley Nelson, Laurens Grant. PBS, 2011. DVD.

When you think about the civil rights time table, this story doesn't seem to fit in with everything else. It had been nearly 100 years since slavery had been outlawed. Nearly 100 years since the remaining 40,000+ slaves were set free. Nearly 100 years since so many of them took on new last names, like *Freeman* or *King* (because they were free men who felt like kings).

But consider the timetable. In 1863 Lincoln gives his famous Emancipation Proclamation speech and declares all slaves free. Two years later, in 1865, Congress passes the Thirteenth Amendment outlawing slavery. Two years between the speech and the law. That's a long time. The wheels of politics turn slowly.

But how slow do the wheels of society turn?

Much.

Much.

Slower.

Two years between the speech and the law, and for the next 100 years black people remain subject to the most shameful, dehumanizing treatment in the United States: separate drinking fountains for whites and "coloreds," separate bathrooms, segregated schools, whites-only restaurants, flaming crosses, and death by hanging for innocent black men and women.

Slavery may have ended in 1863, but a hundred years later the echoes could still be heard loud and clear. The chains of slavery had been broken, but the shadows and scars remained. In the 1960s, African Americans may have had *legal* rights, but they were far from having *civil* rights.

The Supreme Court eventually stepped in with laws to end the discrimination, and in 1960 they outlawed racial segregation on public transportation busses, terminals, and restaurants. But even after the law was in place, blacks were still being mistreated and abused in these very same places.

One group had enough. In Washington DC, a black leader named James Farmer organized a group calling itself CORE - The Congress of Racial Equality. Farmer decided it was time to take action. So he recruited groups of blacks and whites to test the new laws by riding public busses into the deep south. They would boldly face discrimination and perhaps even violence on their journey toward racial reconciliation.

Like Dr. Martin Luther King Jr., the Freedom Riders would embrace a philosophy of nonviolence, committing to turn the other cheek and to never return violence for violence.

What followed was more than anyone expected. Local police organized violent attacks *with* the Ku Klux Klan in Anniston and Birmingham Alabama. When the Freedom Riders arrived at the public bus station in Anniston, they were met by an angry mob. The bus driver tried to pull away, but the mob slashed the tires, lit the bus on fire, and held the doors shut trying to burn them alive.

Local police stood by watching it happen... and they did absolutely nothing to stop it.

When the bus's fuel tank exploded, the mob moved back, and the Freedom Riders poured out of the bus, gasping and choking for air. But before they could get away, the mob moved back in and beat many of them to a bloody pulp until highway patrolmen fired warning shots into the air, and the mob scattered.

The riders received minimal medical treatment before being kicked out of the local hospital, and they continued on to Birmingham, Alabama, where they were met with more violence. They continued on despite the very real threat that in every city, large mobs of ignorant white supremacists would try to kill them.

You would think this level of violence would have sent them packing their bags, heading home for safety. But in fact, it did just the opposite. More Freedom Rides started up at college campuses and churches in the northern states. And facing brutal beatings, false imprisonment, and even death... the rides continued on.

Hundreds of riders were arrested and sent to jail in Jackson, Mississippi, until the jails literally filled up. And all this NOT for breaking the law mind you, but for exercising their legal rights to a civil society where blacks and whites are treated as equal. And guess what?

It worked.

The Freedom Riders ultimately became known for breaking down some of the most hateful discrimination in American history.

All because they decided to stand up and lead.

○ ○ ○

Let's go back to the night that James Farmer recruited the first group of Freedom Riders. Whether the students in the room knew it or not, each of them was living their life in one of four ways: as a **wanderer**, **explorer**, **follower**, or **leader**. That night, they were challenged to become followers of a great vision. A vision to end racism.

The same holds true today. In your school, in your class, on your team, and all around you, people live as wanderers, followers, explorers, and leaders.

# WANDERERS

**Wanderers** are people who have no purpose. They lack the motivation to serve anyone but themselves. Drifting through life without ambition or determination, they fail to see past the present moment. They are unaware of the needs of others, and they live to gratify the immediate desires of their own existence.

Wanderers might talk about their ambitions (Lord knows they love talking about themselves), but their daydreams never come to fruition, as they wait for life to reward them for doing, well... nothing. Some of you are like, *Listen Buddy, playing 5 hours of video games a night isn't nothing! It's an accomplishment!* Uhmm yeah. Keep telling yourself that. While you occupy the couch, the rest of us will be taking ambition, being the change, and rocking the world.

The thing is: most wanderers don't even know they're wandering. They don't know they're missing out on a greater story. They "don't know what they don't know," so they become stuck in perpetual childhood, wandering through life with no purpose.

Fortunately for you, if you've read this far, you are probably already searching for more in life, and that kind of searching is what makes you an explorer.

## EXPLORERS

**Explorers** are searching for their purpose in life. They know they have a unique contribution to make in this world, and they set out on a quest to find it. The key here is going through some trial and error along the way. You cannot find out what you're good at without simultaneously finding out what you're bad at. So don't be afraid of failure. Every failure can bring you one step closer to success – one step closer to discovering what you were made for.

Your Aunt Mimi will always think you can win the next season of American Idol, so find some people who will give you honest feedback about your strengths and weaknesses. Most of the time family and friends are too close to give you the unfiltered criticism you need.

But here's the warning: if your journey of *self*-discovery stays *self*-focused for very long, it can turn into a cycle of *selfishness*. And selfish people rarely find their purpose.

When I was 19 and finishing up my first year of college, I didn't know what I wanted to do. At the time I dreamed of playing music full time, and I wasn't really sure if I should continue with college (that eventually changed, and I got my degree), but before I figured any of that out, I had to go through a season of discovery. I had to become an explorer.

Fortunately, I had a lot of friends who were exploring their own journeys, so we had lots of things to talk about. I took a semester off from school to explore life. The best job I could find was as – get this – a used car salesman. Not exactly glamorous. I had a swank thrift store suit that I wore, and they even gave me business cards. What I learned was this: I can sell cars, but not without selling my soul. According to my boss, every car on our lot had been "owned by a single old lady who drove the car to town and back a few times a week for groceries." When anyone asked about a car's background, we were supposed to tell a version of this tall tale.

The trouble? I have a hard time lying to people, so I just couldn't do it. I worked there for about three months before quitting. Exploring your purpose can be hard, difficult work. I was embarrassed that I hadn't made it in the car business, but at least I still had my integrity intact.

Looking back, was the car gig a complete waste of time? No way. I learned about business, I learned about myself, I stood up for my beliefs, and most importantly, I failed forward – a concept I was reading about at the time in a book by John Maxwell[12]. In other words, by failing forward, I was letting that experience propel me further in my quest. The car gig showed me that life was much bigger than money. It taught me that I needed to be serving a bigger purpose – a purpose bigger than me, myself, and I.

# FOLLOWERS

If you want to move beyond the explorer stage, you have to become a follower. **Followers** are people who find a bigger purpose worth pursuing, a cause worth joining, a dream worth living. They are workers who learn the joy of selfless giving and sacrifice. And as ironic as it may seem,

---

[12] Maxwell, John C.. Failing Forward. Nashville, TN: Nelson Publishers, 2000.

becoming a good follower is one of the key factors in predicting your future success as a leader.

A lot of people get stuck in a never-ending explorer stage because, even when they find a purpose, they still focus on themselves, so they fail to grow into leaders. They may even go as far as starting a business, declaring a vision, and hiring some staff. But no one wants to follow them. Why? Because selfish purposes reek like dog farts. I don't know any other way to say it. Everyone hates the smell except the dog itself, who remains completely unaware.

If your goals are no bigger than you, people will sniff you out. You can try to mask it with clever marketing and fancy search engine optimization, but you can't fool human beings on this one. It's in our blood to follow noble purposes, to dream bigger dreams, to live a greater story.

Your dog, on the other hand, will follow you anywhere. But why trust him? I mean, really, he can't even smell his own farts.

## LEADERS

**Leaders** embrace a greater purpose, one that focuses on making life better for other people. It's a purpose bigger than themselves. The best leaders are also the best followers. From a distance, you may not even see who or what they are following, but get closer and it becomes very clear. Great leaders are always searching for new ways to grow. They devour resources that will satisfy their love of learning and quench their thirst for wisdom. They pull inspiration from books, magazines, the internet, and strangers sitting next to them on airplanes. They listen to people who work underneath them and people of different social status. They seek advice from experts and mentors who have more life experience than them. In short, they are sponges of wisdom, sucking it up wherever they can find it.

A Leader is a giver – someone with a passionate purpose for serving people. They find their cause, and that drives them to want to develop other people around them, perhaps for the same cause, but often with no agenda at all other than the joy of contributing to someone else's growth in life.

We respect great leaders because we trust that they have ***everyone's best interests at heart***. We follow them because they have a crystal clear purpose to serve a noble cause.

A clear purpose, and a fight worth fighting for, these are the beginning roots of a great leader and the foundations of the **TEEN LEADERSHIP REVOLUTION**.

# CHAPTER FOUR STUDY GUIDE

7. Why do you think the Freedom Riders were motivated to stand up and step out as leaders?

8. Of the four types of people (Wanderers, Explorers, Followers, and Leaders), which do you think best describes where you are at personally? Why?

9. Why do you think so many teens get stuck in a never ending "explorer cycle?"

10. What are some of the unseen ways that the best leaders are also the best followers?

11. In the space below, write out one thing you could do to focus your mind and to reach the next level as a leader.

12. Write the name of one person and one resource (book, blog, etc.) you can follow to grow as a leader.

# CHAPTER FIVE

# FOUR LEVELS OF LEADERSHIP

Have you ever noticed there is a big difference between having the title of "leader" and being the actual leader of a group? We all know who the official leader is, but who is the unofficial leader? Who has the most influence in the group? I call this being the "perceived leader." What do I mean by that?

If a group of non-English speaking people observed your group and couldn't understand one word that was said, who would they say the leader is? Who would they *perceive* to be the leader? In the best groups, the official leader is also the perceived leader, but in many teams this is not the case. You can see it in the eyes of the group members. Who captures every eye in the room when they talk? Who does everyone look at during the critical moments? Most of the time, this person is the perceived leader. Like it or not, the perceived leader is the most influential person in the room. That doesn't mean they're always the loudest, the most talkative, or the most prepared. But when they speak, everyone listens.

Perceived leadership isn't given by title, or won through elections. It is earned over time through relationships, results, and respect.

○ ○ ○

Jessica was Student Council President, a title she had won decisively in the school election. She was well prepared and focused for the student council meetings, but other than having the support of the Treasurer (her best friend Alison), she could not gain traction with the rest of the team. After one meeting, she noticed a couple of team members having a sidebar conversation (also known as a "meeting after the meeting"). They were second guessing a decision the group had made during the meeting. This made Jessica very frustrated, and she wanted to quit. *Why wouldn't they voice their concerns during the meeting? Why wouldn't they support the groups' decision over their own agenda?* These questions echoed through her brain.

Jessica was the official leader, but she wasn't the perceived leader of the group... at least not yet.

There are four levels of leadership that every leader must move through *with their group* to achieve the highest level of success. These unseen levels of leadership are the keys to victory or defeat with any team. Leaders who consistently climb the levels, bringing their teammates with them along the way, achieve real success and satisfaction with their group.

## LEADERSHIP BY RIGHTS

The first level is **Leadership by Rights**. In Jessica's case, she is the official Student Council President. She alone holds the rights to that office. She has the right to schedule meetings, to make the agenda, and to set the course of action for the school year. She can even invoke these rights by demanding that her team follows her. But if she demands her rights as the leader, what will happen? Most likely she will accomplish the exact opposite goal – her teammates will either quit, revolt, or follow her with bad attitudes. In the real world, Leadership By Rights doesn't get you very far. You know why? *Because I'm the boss, that's why! I'm the boss, and you can follow me or lose your job. Blah blah blah.* No one wants to follow this kind of leadership for obvious reasons, but they do so for fear of being fired, embarrassed, or kicked off the team.

## LEADERSHIP BY RELATIONSHIPS

The second level is **Leadership by Relationships**. Jessica's best friend is Alison, the Student Council Treasurer. To Alison, Jessica is more than the President of the Student

Council; she is also a true friend. There is no mystery to why the one girl follows the other. Alison and Jessica have a great relationship, so they make great teammates. The second level of leadership says that if people like you (and more importantly, if they know you like them), then they will follow you. In school elections, this can sometimes be the deciding factor behind who wins the race and who goes home defeated. The underlying belief is that people who like us will make decisions that are in our best interests. We trust you. You are our friend.

Good leaders understand this principle, so they do everything they can to build trust in their groups. They listen. They ask questions. They hold teambuilding events. They care for their teammates, knowing that authentic relationships are the foundation for the group's eventual success. Great leaders go deep with people, knowing that it strengthens the team and builds trust.

The danger at this level is that some leaders get stuck in relationship mode, and they cannot move beyond it. They want to be wanted, need to be needed (what psychologists call "codependency"). They try to please all the people all the time, so they change their views with the pulse of popular opinion. They become like politicians who are forever running for office. Ironically, this is what erodes trust in their team, the very thing they are trying so hard to build.

# LEADERSHIP BY RESULTS

A high level leader learns to take the team beyond the relationship level by adding the third level of leadership: **Leadership by Results.** In this level, the teammates begin to trust the track record of the leader. They see all the hard work and all the discipline, and it proves to them that the leader has the group's best interests at heart, even when it is unpopular.

Leadership by Results is risky business. You have to be secure enough to make the tough call, to cast the tie-breaking vote, and to stand firm when necessary. Along the way, you learn that real success cannot be attained without risking real failure. I would even go further, saying that real success is only obtained by walking through real failure.

Successful people DO NOT have a "better batting average" at life. They don't hit homeruns all the time – not even most of the time. In fact, most successful people are often the ones who have failed the most along the way. But they keep stepping up to the plate, back into the batter's box of life, knowing that every failure brings them closer to success. They trade real risk for real reward.

The reality is there is no shortcut to success. Leadership by Results doesn't happen in a microwave, it cooks slowly in the crockpot. For Jessica to lead by results, she has to prove herself time and again with high consistency and high accountability. She has to earn her stripes.

# LEADERSHIP BY RESPECT

But here's the cool part. When you lead by relationships and by results, you can eventually be propelled into the highest level of leadership: **Leadership by Respect.** Again, you've been bringing your team with you along the way. They like you, and they like your results, so they begin to trust your judgment. They begin to respect you as a leader, and that means they will value your opinions and contributions even when they disagree with you. To be clear, it doesn't mean they will always agree with you, but it means they will always respect you.

In the first level, you are given *rights*, and people follow you if they have to. In the second level, you build *relationships*, and people follow because they believe you have their personal best interests at heart. In the third level, you start to develop a track record of good *results*, and people follow because they believe you have the best interests of the team in mind. And in the final level, people follow you because they *respect* you, trusting that you have everyone's best interests at heart.

Now for the special sauce. Did you notice that you can do levels two, three, and four without ever being given the official title of "leader? "It's true. And this is the challenge that 95% of leaders find themselves in. They want to lead, but they don't have the official title. The temptation is to sit back and be quiet until someone calls on you. The temptation is to be passive-aggressive. The temptation is to have a meeting after the meeting, or to say things like, "Well, I wouldn't have done it that way."

The reality is this. We need unofficial leaders to speak up. We need perceived leaders to step up. We need team players who will shoulder the load of leadership and serve the group over their own special interests.

You listen. You learn. You serve others before yourself. This is how you build a **TEEN LEADERSHIP REVOLUTION**.

# CHAPTER FIVE STUDY GUIDE

1. Who do you think is the "perceived leader" in one of your groups? Why is that person seen as the leader?

2. Why do you think Jessica's teammates were having a "meeting after the meeting?"

3. What are some creative things Jessica could have done to improve the relationships within her team?

4. What level of leadership best describes where you are at: Rights, Relationship, Results, or Respect?

5. What do you think is the main thing that separates Leadership by Results from Leadership by Respect?

6. What do you need to do to move toward the next level in your leadership?

# CHAPTER SIX

## SELF-DISCIPLINE

Once a week I mentor a 4th grade kid named Jimmy. He comes from a broken home, and he struggles in school, so I meet with him each week for a one-hour mentoring session. Recently I said to Jimmy, "Jimmy, do you know how character is built?" He said no. I said "with self-discipline." Then I asked him, "Jimmy, do you know what self-discipline is?" He sighed and said, "Sounds like hurting yourself." And with that, he proceeded to jam his pencil into his leg! I was like, "Ah!... Don't do that!"

I said, "No, not so much. Self-discipline is actually a good thing. It's self-correcting to make your own life better."

Discipline is not something you can avoid. You can either be self-disciplined or *you will be* disciplined by others. You can self-correct, or *you will be* corrected by others. It's crazy when you think about it - in America we have a whole department devoted to correcting people who do not correct themselves. It's called the Department of Corrections. Yes, the Department of Corrections - PRISON. It's where you go when you have no self-discipline, so you have to be disciplined by others.

Every time I look at my phone, I see the background photo of me and Jimmy, and I'm reminded of this principle. In the photo he's wearing an orange shirt that says "OUT ON BAIL." It's designed to look like a prison inmate shirt. And every time I see it, I think to myself *"that's why I'm doing this – to keep Jimmy from wearing the real life version of that shirt!"*

I always tell Jimmy that one of the signs of maturity is being able to delay satisfaction. In other words, if you're self-disciplined, you can force yourself to wait to get something good. You can make yourself work hard and be patient until you ultimately earn something of value.

When Jimmy and I first began meeting two years ago, I would try to give him opportunities to learn this principle, so I would present him with crazy choices. I would say thing like:

> *Jimmy, today we can play board games for ten minutes, then do homework for the rest of the hour, OR... we can do homework for twenty minutes, then play board games for the rest of the hour. Which do you choose?*

In the first scenario Jimmy would get ten minutes of games, and in the second scenario he would get forty minutes of games. A pretty obvious choice right? Not so much. Jimmy could not delay the satisfaction of playing games, so he would choose the ten minutes of instant fun, only to follow it with fifty minutes of grueling homework.

Astonishing. The power of instant satisfaction completely takes over. We want. We want it bad. We want it now.

○ ○ ○

We face decisions like this every day don't we? We choose to spend time on facebook or youtube, so we can procrastinate and delay doing our homework. *Why do today what I can put off until tomorrow?* This is the motto of many teens.

And maybe it's becoming your motto. Even if you never say it with your mouth, are you saying it with your life?

The problem with instant satisfaction is that it distracts you from your real focus. The ten minutes online turns into thirty. By then you've forgotten all about your homework. The thirty minutes turns into a whole evening, and before you know it you're slapping together your homework in the class period before it is due.

Problems like this don't go away on their own. They actually grow and fester and turn into monsters that live under your bed and eat little kittens, which are considered a delicacy to monsters.

Each morning when your feet hit the floor, you have a choice. You can feed the monster of procrastination and laziness or you can kick him in the face and ban him from your life. In most cases, a single banning won't do because the monster is so persistent.

Maybe it's all the kittens you've been feeding him.

I'm joking, but there is a lot of truth to that. Old habits really do die hard. If you are caught in a cycle of laziness or procrastination, there is really only one way to kill the beast within, and that is with self-discipline.

## SELF-DISCIPLINE IS THE ENGINE THAT DRIVES CHARACTER.

Without self-discipline your life drifts into the dark waters of self-destruction. You start to float in any direction except where you actually want to go, and the worst part is just drifting along realizing that you are completely out of fuel. You're stuck. You're going nowhere fast.

But it doesn't have to be that way.

○ ○ ○

The key to developing self-discipline is finding something worth living for. Something worth fighting for. When I returned home from the Burdick farm all those years ago,

I remember walking into my room and seeing it there – my first electric guitar. My parents knew I had been learning to play, so they bought it for me as a surprise. When I saw it I totally flipped out! I had been learning on my mom's old classical guitar, and this thing was way better.

It might only have been a cheap knockoff of a Fender Stratocaster, but it felt like the best guitar in the world. Cause it was mine.

I began practicing every day for hours on end. I used music as a way of releasing all the pent-up emotions I had inside. I finally had a reason to work hard, a reason for some self-discipline.

A few weeks later I formed a band with my friend Brent the bass player, and a couple weeks after that we recruited Matt the drummer. In the months that followed we enlisted my sister Andrea the singer and our friend Dan the keyboardist. We decided to hold practice every Saturday from 8am to noon.

In the past I never liked getting up early on the weekends. Now it was easy, a no-brainer. I knew if we ever wanted to get gigs and record our own music, we would need a solid dose of self-discipline to make it happen.

So for the next three and a half years we busted our butts for the band. We started by playing free shows for whoever would listen, and over time we began getting paid to play. Before we broke-up and went to college we were getting up to $800 a gig, which was a lot back then. That would be like eleventy-thousand dollars in today's money.

We worked hard and we used the benchmark of self-discipline to elevate us to new levels as a band. While we were together we saw a lot of other local bands come and go. Some were better musicians than us. Most had nicer instruments than us. But none of them were as focused, as committed, or as disciplined as us. And it showed over time.

○ ○ ○

For decades, infomercials have advertised weight loss programs that are "quick and easy," claiming things like, "You can have the perfect body in just three minutes a day." The videos are full of smiling skinny people who look like they're having an absolute blast. *(Where do they find these people?)* Over the years, programs like these came and went, but not many of them caught on. This was the traditional thinking for weight loss programs: *make a program look fun and easy, and people will buy it.*

But then something new happened. A guy named Tony Horton started marketing his weight loss program with the complete opposite message. Tony's program was advertised as a 90-day boot camp in your own living room. He was the drill sergeant, and the marketing message was clear: Tony was going to charge you $120 to scream at you through your own TV. He was going to work your own butt off... literally. Guess whose program sold millions of copies and actually worked for millions of people? Yep, Tony's program... more commonly known as P90X[13].

Not to be outdone, Shaun Thompson ("Shaun T") developed an "insane" workout program that was supposed to be harder than P90X. He claimed it was *"the only workout that will leave you face down in a puddle of your own sweat!"* (A direct quote from the infomercial.)

*A puddle of my own sweat, you say? Yes pleeeease!!!!!* And since Insanity and P90X were both owned by the same company, Beachbody, they shared the same price point. Yes, *I'd love to pay you another $120 to scream at me through my own TV.*

The crazy thing is: it worked. Many of the same P90X customers shelled out another $120 to get Insanity. Why did it work? The answer is obvious: truth in advertising... the program's claims are true: If you work out until you lay in a pool of your own sweat, YOU WILL LOSE WEIGHT.

People resonated with the P90X and Insanity messages because they knew it was true – the only way to lose weight fast and build muscle is to do an insane workout. (And after this chapter, both of these programs should start sending me a commission check.)

---

[13] Rovell, Darren. "Beachbody's P90X Making Serious Money" CNBC.com. N.p., 9 June 2010. Web. <http://www.cnbc.com/>.

So... truth in advertising: If you want to build character, you have to have self-discipline, but not just with your physical body. You also have to practice self-discipline with your heart and mind. You must take control of your complete being, day after day, week after week. And sadly, I will not be marketing my own video program to scream at you through your own, TV telling you to GET OFF YOUR BUTT AND DO YOUR HOMEWORK!!! PLAN THE BIG EVENT! ASK HER OUT!!! DO SOMETHING NICE FOR YOUR PARENTS.

You'll have to tell those things to yourself. After all, it is called *self*-discipline for a reason.

You see, self-discipline is not something you choose to do today and it's done. It is not something you can commit to for the next two weeks. No. It is something you choose every day. It's a way of living that says *"I want something so bad I'm willing to kick myself in the butt until I make it happen."*

So how good are you at kicking yourself in the butt? This is the measure of your self-discipline.

# CHAPTER SIX STUDY GUIDE

1. Rate yourself on a scale of one to ten, with ten being the best. How are you doing with self-discipline in your life?

2. In what area of your life are you having the hardest time with self-discipline?

3. At what times of the day are you most likely to slip into laziness and procrastination?

4. What is one positive step you could take today to improve your self-discipline?

5. CHALLENGE: Get up twenty minutes early tomorrow morning and discipline yourself to do something positive before you go to school. Write your plan in the space below.

## CHAPTER SEVEN

## RESPONSIBILITY

Responsibility is an easy word to figure out. Response-ability: it's your ability to respond. Are you response-able?

As long as you're alive, you always have the ability to respond. When you're dead you lose this ability. I guess you could say dead people are completely irresponsible... because they're dead. So until you die, **your response is your responsibility.**

If you take one thing away from this chapter, take this:

## OWN YOUR LIFE.

This is the essence of responsibility.

An owner is someone who takes responsibility for their *own* choices and actions. Even when they mess up, they don't make excuses. They own it.

So I'm watching the news the other night and a group of reporters are just hammering these two military generals. They're irate over some breach of security in Afghanistan. I barely even remember what it's all about because I'm completely stunned by the head general's response. The reporters push harder, "Whose fault is this? Who is *responsible* for this massive breach of security?!!"

The general stops, looks right at them, and says in a calm voice, "You're looking at him. I am."

Whaaa??? He just sat there and took responsibility for the whole thing? Unreal. I mean, there were so many other excuses he could have made. The general wasn't the actual person who messed up. It was obviously an officer under him – probably several levels under him. I bet he didn't even know who did it, but he stood there and took full responsibility. On live TV. Before the whole world.

It left the reporters speechless. He owned it.

○ ○ ○

"It wasn't my fault!" "I had no choice!" It is much more common to hear this kind of language. These are the slogans of "victims" who know nothing of responsibility. It's as if outside forces are responsible for all the bad things that happen in their life. They certainly aren't responsible for it – they are the victims of it. When things go good, they're the first to take credit, but when things go bad, they're the last to accept blame.

They become professional blame-shifters. When blame shows up on their front porch, they simply move to a different house. *Let's just shift this blame over here, over there, anywhere!* Blame is a hot potato that many people cannot handle because they simply refuse to own it.

Students who refuse to own their lives end up making excuses for everything. Sometimes it gets pretty silly, as they shift the blame to anyone but themselves. Take homework, for example. Over the years I've collected homework excuses and put them in my list of **THE TOP 10 HOMEWORK EXCUSES OF ALL TIME**. See if any of these sound familiar...

1. My dog ate my homework (aka "The Classic").
2. I have a solar powered calculator, but it was cloudy day.
3. Timmy fell into a lake, so I jumped in to rescue him! ...Sadly my homework drowned.
4. I accidentally dropped my homework in the toilet, and somehow it got flushed.
5. I gave my homework to a homeless man to line his hat with – for warmth.
6. The internet was down, my computer crashed, and the printer broke all at the same time!
7. My great aunt died last night, so we spent the rest of the night planning her funeral.

8. I made a paper airplane out of my homework, but it got hijacked.
9. I put my homework in the safe, but I lost the combination.
10. My little brother threw up all over my homework... It was nasty.

Some of these excuses might have even happened to you. Perhaps your little brother actually did puke on your homework. Whose responsibility is that? Did he take you hostage and demand to use your homework as his barf-bag? I'm hoping the answer to that is no. If the answer is yes, then you have more problems than being irresponsible. Also, your brother needs some Tums.

○ ○ ○

## TIPS AND TRICKS

As a student, one of your main responsibilities is to do your homework. Here are some tips and tricks for getting it done and turning it in on time.

The default temptation is to try to remember everything in your head. For example, throughout the school day, you are assigned homework in math, science, and history. You try to remember the list in your head, then you find yourself panicking the next day at school when you realize you totally forgot.

My first tip is to get that list out of your head into a place where it can be collected.

In his book, *Getting Things Done*[14], David Allen describes this as a "bucket." If something is important but cannot be completed in two minutes or less, then you put it into your bucket. Obviously we're not talking about a literal bucket; we're talking about creating a place for collecting all your upcoming assignments and appointments. This could be a notebook, a computer, or even a handheld device like a phone or an iPod. Many schools provide students with a planner or a calendar for this very use. Any assignment that cannot be done immediately gets collected in your bucket.

**TIP 1:** *Get a bucket and begin collecting all your assignments in it.*

**TIP 2:** *Set an alarm.*

The key to Tip 2 is to setup an auto-reminder for what's in your bucket. You can leave your backpack by the door as a reminder, put a piece of paper on your pillow, tie a string on your finger, or even write something on your hand! You can go high-tech and set a reminder on your phone, computer, or iPad. The sky is the limit, so find what works for you.

Responsibility means being honest with yourself and setting a reminder before you forget... because you know you will forget.

---

[14] Allen, David. Getting Things Done: The Art of Stress-Free Productivity. New York: Viking, 2001.

Here's how I do it. My bucket is my notebook and my computer. The first question I ask myself is: "Can I do this in the next two minutes?" If the answer is yes, I do it immediately and get it out of the way (so I don't even collect it in my bucket). If the answer is no, then it goes in one of two places. Anything I need to get done today goes in my notebook on my list of tasks for the day. Everything else goes into my online calendar. I even setup auto-reminders to pop up before the events are due. For smaller tasks (things that take less than an hour) I set a popup reminder for the night before.

The point is: get it out of your brain and into your bucket, then setup a reminder for your bucket. What I love about this method is that it allows me to forget about it! This is a huge stress reliever. The bucket remembers for me, so I don't have to.

Let's face it: homework can be about as much fun as giving your eye a paper cut, but only one of those things will hurt you. So if you're unsure, try them both and get back to me. If you find yourself blaming everyone else for everything else in your life, then it's time to start taking responsibility. Your attitude must be, *"If I don't like my current situation, then it is up to me to make it better."*

The world is full of excuse-makers and buck-passers, but a responsible person is hard to find. If you can learn to accept responsibility for your choices, your actions, and your happiness, you will become something very valuable and rare... a person who truly owns their life.

# CHAPTER SEVEN STUDY GUIDE

1. Rate yourself on a scale of one to ten, with ten being the best. How are you doing with responsibility?

2. In what areas of your life are you most likely to be irresponsible?

3. If you were put on the spot for missing a homework assignment, what would be your natural response? Accept the blame, shift the blame, make excuses, or maybe disappear?

4. What is one positive step you could take today to take charge of your life and to be an owner?

5. CHALLENGE: Next time you are held responsible for something, make absolutely no excuses. Accept the blame and take full responsibility. You will be surprised how this earns you respect - the subject of our next benchmark.

# CHAPTER EIGHT

## RESPECT

Darren was 16 when he hacked into the school's grading system. He wasn't trying to give himself all A's. He was simply trying to prove a point. He changed the scores for one single test; it was a history exam that every kid in class thought was too difficult and unfair. He didn't just change his grade; he gave perfect scores to all his friends – a regular Robin Hood of the computer hacking scene. Things were going great until he got caught. He and his friends received failing grades and a temporary vacation from school. Even worse, they lost the respect of their parents and teachers.

When Darren told me this story, it was clear that the root problem was not the dishonesty of his crime (to be clear, that *was* a problem, just not the biggest problem). Darren's cheating was only an outer sign of an inner problem. Darren's problem was respect. Or to put it more clearly, disrespect. He didn't care what the teachers thought, what his parents would think, or what the consequences were. He wanted to *stick it to the man* and make a public point that the test was unfair. He had absolutely no appreciation for all the work and all the dedication the teacher put in day after day. He wanted to put the teacher in his place.

Darren wasn't a punk kid; he was a disrespectful kid.

The core virtue behind respect is valuing all lives and appreciating all the people who came before us, whose shoulders we now stand on. It is being grateful for every advantage we are born into and for every privilege we are given.

## RESPECT IS ACCEPTING THE DEBT OF GRATITUDE AND HONOR THAT WE OWE THE WORLD –EVEN WHEN WE DON'T FEEL LIKE IT.

When I speak at schools I often ask for a show of hands for how many people know the first name of one of the custodians in their school. If 10% - 20% of the audience raises their hands, it's a good day. Even in the best cases, the vast majority of students do not know the first name of a single janitor in their school. Why is that?

The quick answer is we do not respect what we do not know. The more complicated answer is we make assumptions about people based on their job, clothes, hair, skin color, voice, you name it. We group these assumptions into categories called "stereotypes." Think about how society, television, and the internet stereotype the janitor profession. The unsaid message is that janitors are not smart, not interesting, not clean, and not worth talking to.

Even with the disrespect that surrounds professions like custodians, lunch ladies, fast food workers, and trash collectors, they still willingly serve us day-in and day-out cleaning up the puke in the cafeteria, serving us French Fries, and picking up the trash at the curb.

What kind of assumptions are you making about the people who fly under the radar of your life? What about the people who have authority in your life, like teachers and parents?

It's easy to respect people who are just like us. We hang out with the same friends, we like the same bands, we dress the same, we look the same. But it is more difficult to respect the unknown – people who are different than us. The cool thing is that when we get to know people, we find that we have much more in common than we first thought. Although we humans have vast differences on the outside, we share huge similarities on the inside. We face the same fears, battle the same insecurities, have the same hopes, and dream the same dreams. We all want our lives to matter.

As a teen, that didn't click with me. I didn't respect my teachers until they earned it, and I assumed they were doing the same for me. Since I had no respect for myself, I had almost none for anyone else. It was a vicious cycle that led me down a dark path. Thank God I am not the person I used to be.

So what changed?

When I was on the Burdick's farm they taught me that I would only get as much respect as I gave to others. Since I gave none, I received none in return. I remember being late one morning as I was getting ready for school, and Mr. Burdick let me have it. He said,

> Son, you are not being respectful of Mrs. Burdick's time. When you are late, it's like telling the other person that your time is more important than their time! Do you do this to your mother at home? Your mother went into the bowels of death to bring you to life, so you owe nothing less than your utmost respect and honor.

At the time I thought he was being a bit overdramatic (what on earth are the *"bowels of death"* anyway?), but over time, his comments rang true.

My parents don't have to earn my respect; I owe it to them by default. The same thing with my teachers and with any person of authority.

The key is understanding where respect is due and where respect is earned. As a student, you give respect to others but you earn in for yourself.

THAT'S NOT FAIR, you say?

Yep, you're right, it's not fair. But respect isn't built on fairness. Respect is built on accepting the debt of gratitude and honor that you owe this world for the gift of life itself.

# CHAPTER EIGHT STUDY GUIDE

1. Rate yourself on a scale of one to ten, with ten being the best. How are you doing with respect toward your parents, teachers, friends, and even to yourself?

2. In the last week where have you been the most respectful? Teachers, Parents, Yourself? Where have you struggled with disrespect?

3. Give yourself a do-over. Think of a recent time when you were disrespectful, and write what you will do differently in the future.

4. Write down one relationship in your life where respect is *due* and another one where it is *earned*. What are some of the differences you see?

5. CHALLENGE: Find the person(s) you were disrespectful to and offer a sincere apology. Let them know you're working on being more respectful, and do something kind for them to show your sincerity.

# CHAPTER NINE

# HONESTY

As I gazed out the window the buildings below got smaller and smaller until they disappeared entirely. I was 18, and it was my first time flying. Me, my debate partner Nathan, and our debate coach were headed to Arkansas for a state-wide debate tournament. We had done well in Michigan, we had placed second in Ohio, and now we planned to take Arkansas by storm.

The Arkansas kids talked funny with their southern drawl accents. I remember them saying we had accents too, but I couldn't hear it. They said the Michigan accent was squeaky, like someone talking while pinching their nose. Whatever. We were there to win, not talk about stupid accents. I didn't care if I ever saw these kids again. It was go-time, time to win.

Now, if you've never witnessed a high school debate tournament, it is quite the sight. At the beginning of the school year you are given a debate topic, ours was "Campaign Finance Reform" (exciting – I know). At each debate, you come prepared to argue for either side of the issue, and you don't find out which side until right before the match when the judges flip a coin. It's a lot like the National Football League when you think about it... except for the actual hitting part, and the cheering fans part, and the football part.

So you come prepared to argue for both the affirmative – meaning you say the system should change, or the negative – meaning you want to keep the status quo.

Nathan and I were on a roll, winning debates on either side of the issue. The only challenge was that the local Arkansas teams kept using this one particular quote. The quote was good. The quote was solid. It was from a senator. It was hard evidence, and it was hard to debate against.

The local teams shared the same debate coach, so they all had this same "super-quote" as their prime piece of evidence, and it kept biting us. We knew if we could just find a way to destroy their evidence, we would be invincible, flying our way to the final round with ease. So after the first day of the tournament we searched far and wide for evidence to combat their super-quote. Thanks to Google we found exactly what they were using. We had the whole manuscript. It was from a speech given by some senator on Capitol Hill, but we had nothing to contradict it, no opposite piece of evidence to use against them.

Suddenly, Nathan and I had a bright idea. What if we used selective parts of the quote to make it say what we wanted it to say? We wouldn't jumble the quote or make anything up; we would just stop the quote mid-sentence, so it appeared to be in our favor. We wondered aloud if there was a problem with our plan. Would the judges care if we only used half a quote? The senator still said those words, didn't he? Of course he did, so it was a real quote from the senator. End of story. We needed a solution, and we found it.

The next day we made it to the semi-finals before facing super-quote. Out of all the teams in the tournament, we were in the final four, which meant half of the tournament was now watching our debate. We sat behind a small table facing the crowd and a panel of three judges. It was nerve wrecking.

Our opponents came out swinging, presenting a plan so crystal clear it practically reeked of Windex. And you guessed it, they used super-quote. It rolled off their tongue like the silver bullet of death.

Super-quote was threatening to undue us. It was kicking us while we were down. Minutes felt like hours as we waited for our turn to speak. Finally, it was time for Operation Half-Quote Trickery. As I approached the podium, I felt a little dishonest, but who had time to think about honesty? We wanted to win. I believe I already established that.

Nathan and I proceeded to use a selection of half-quotes and half-truths to prove our point. And we did a pretty good job of it, to tell you the truth. We were convincing, like real politicians. Everything was going as planned. But what we didn't plan for was about to happen, and that would change everything.

When the other team came up for the questioning round they asked us if we had used half-quotes to mislead the judges. We dodged the question. They asked us if we had purposely ended the quotes mid-sentence to make them portray the opposite meaning. We bumbled out something about how the words we used were actually from the manuscript.

And then it happened... something we didn't expect or even think possible.

The judges actually stopped the debate and asked to see the evidence. Could they even do that? The answer was yes. They were the judges. They could do anything.

My heart sank into the souls of my shoes. And even from way down there I could feel my heartbeat pounding in my throat.

The judges walked out of the room to review the evidence.

Time.

Stood.

Still.

I wanted to cry. I knew we had been dishonest.

The judges came back in the room and announced that the debate was over. We were immediately disqualified for attempting to deceive the judges.

I was pretty sure they were going to give us the death penalty; send us right to the electric chair. But they didn't. And in seconds, our debate hopes were shattered.

As I raised my head to look at the judges, I forced myself to say, "You made the right decision."

And they had.

The other team went on to the finals, and we went home disgraced. Completely humiliated.

IT WAS A HIGH PRICE TO PAY FOR A LESSON ON HONESTY, BUT SOMETIMES LIFE HAS TO JOLT YOU AWAKE WITH THE TRUTH. THERE'S NOTHING LIKE CONSEQUENCES TO HELP YOU UNDERSTAND REALITY.

If I could take back that one moment, I would. I don't mean the moment when we used the half-quote. I mean the moment when we decided to use it... the night before. When we made that one small decision, it was all over from there. I could have stood up for what was right. I could have listened to my conscience. But I didn't. I wanted to win, even if it cost me everything.

Thankfully, I'm not the same person I used to be. I changed, one choice at a time. And a series of right choices leads to right habits, leads to rock solid character.

○ ○ ○

No one likes to think of themselves as a cheater. It's always "the other people" who do the cheating. But the fact is, in the average American high school, 90% of the student population will admit to cheating in a given school year. That means four out of five teens reading this book admit to cheating in school. Are you in the vast majority or the small minority?

The problem with dishonesty is that it breeds more... dishonesty. When you start a lie, it always takes more lies to keep the first one going. And when you justify dishonesty in small things, you will justify it in bigger things down the road.

What kind of a person are you if you cannot be trusted? Trust is like a wall that takes a long time to build up but only a moment to knock down.

Being honest is absolutely worth it. Even if it costs you something big in the short run (like losing a debate or failing a test), it will pay you back in the long run. Honesty will win you the respect of your teachers, the pride of your parents, and the trust of your friends.

Students of character know this, and they are proactive about living an honest, trustworthy life.

So how are you doing with honesty? Are you a trustworthy person? Use the study guide on the next page to make a growth plan for this principle.

# CHAPTER NINE STUDY GUIDE

1. Why do you think it is so easy to be dishonest?

2. In what area of your life are you having the hardest time with honesty? Where is it easiest to be dishonest?

3. How many friends would consider you a trustworthy person? Do you have your parents' trust? What about your teachers? How can you begin to build trust into these relationships?

4. What is one positive step you could take today to improve your honesty and trustworthiness?

5. CHALLENGE: Identify a time when you have been dishonest. Write it down. Now write out a plan to come forth with the truth and make things right.

# '10

## CHAPTER TEN

## FAIRNESS

Every Tuesday in downtown Grand Rapids Michigan a group of more than 200 homeless people gather at Veteran's Memorial Park. They arrive for what the locals call "Homeless Hotdog Tuesday." I know what you're thinking: *Hotdogs can't be homeless!* You're right, they can't. Stop distracting me – that's not the point.

How could a whole group of people go without adequate housing and food week after week, year after year? I wondered about this from a distance until one Tuesday I kicked myself in the butt and went to the park to see if I could help out. The volunteers put me to work quickly and I was assigned to the drink station. The plastic cups of lemonade were so small; I must have filled over 200 of them to quench the crowd's thirst.

Most of the people seemed truly happy. They called me "Sir" and gave me a tremendous amount of respect. I kept wondering about their personal stories. Did they grow up in poverty? How did they become homeless? Why don't they have jobs? Do they have kids? These questions hung in my mind.

I continued volunteering every Tuesday, and two weeks later I met Marcel, a 46 year old African American man. He hung out near my lemonade stand and simply commented on the weather. We made chit chat to break the ice, and before I knew it, I was voicing aloud the questions that rang in my head.

Marcel was very candid telling me who he was and where he came from. He had grown up in tough circumstances, without ever knowing his father. He was the middle child of three siblings with an older brother and a younger sister.

One afternoon, Marcel's mother left him and his two siblings home while she went shopping. She told the older brother, who was 13, to watch the younger two: Marcel who was six, and Tasha who was four.

While the older brother napped on the couch, Marcel and Tasha went upstairs and climbed the ladder to go explore the attic. At six and four, they didn't think twice to start playing with an old book of matches that they found in a pile of dusty newspapers.

Before they knew it, a spark ignited the papers, and flames jumped up into the rafters. They raced down the ladder screaming for the older brother. Marcel darted down the stairs and out the front door thinking Tasha was fast on his heels. The older brother met him in the front yard and began screaming at him. Where was Tasha? Nobody knew.

When the fire was finally put out, the firefighters combed through the remains of the house until they found Tasha. She had run to the safest place she knew – under her bed. And that's where they found her, her lifeless body lying there charred by the flames.

An absolute tragedy. Completely unfair.

I stood there listening while Marcel explained how his mother had always blamed him for her death. I asked if they had ever reconciled over the years, and he said no. Imagine that: thirty-plus years of living with that kind of guilt, and from your own mother no less. Your chances at living a successful life would be greatly reduced growing up under the weight of guilt and shame.

I asked Marcel if there was anything I could do to help him reconcile with him mother. He reached into his pocket and pulled out a Ziploc bag. In it were two photos: the only two photos of Tasha that sill existed, cracked and weathered from years of wear. One picture was her newborn photo from the hospital, and the other was her funeral photo: a tiny, beautiful girl in a tiny casket.

The only two photos left… her birthday and her death day. Marcel said his mother hadn't seen the photos for over 30 years.

Something inside me jumped. My heart pulsed from the emotion of the story, and my mind raced about how I could help out.

"Marcel," I said, "If you can trust me to take these photos for two weeks, I will bring them back fully restored with copies for you and your mom." He hesitated to accept my gift, but graciously gave in, and I left with the pictures.

Two weeks later I show up at the park wearing my work clothes (fancypants, button-up shirt, dress shoes, a real professional), and I'm carrying a manila envelope in my hand. Then I see Marcel crossing the street to the park.

Now, you have to understand, Marcel usually wears "normal" clothes: jeans, t-shirts, regular stuff. But on this day he shows up wearing a black leather jacket, black do-rag, black pants, and sunglasses. And here he comes to meet up with mister fancypants (aka, me), and exchange a manila envelope in Veteran's Memorial Park! I'm thinking, *Oh yeah, this looks really good.* I'm just waiting for the cops to make the first arrest in world history for photo restoration.

The awkward moment subsided when Marcel pulled the newly restored photos from the envelope. He was speechless with a tear in his eye. He asked how much he owed me, and said, "Nothing at all. I just want you to have a chance to reconcile with your mother, and now you have a way to do it." We hugged, and I encouraged him to make sure and have the conversation.

The next time I saw Marcel he was smiling ear to ear. It was like watching a new person – a person who had been relived from a great burden. He was practically walking on air, dropping jokes about the weather and local politics. He was finally free.

○ ○ ○

What I learned from Marcel was this. No matter how unfair your life is, there will always be people who have it worse. And comparing your life to those who have it "better" or "worse" will always seem unfair. Life is like that. It deals a different set of cards to each of us, and we get to choose how to play them.

Fairness is ultimately about recognizing unfairness. You recognize it, and then you do something about it.

Fairness means acknowledging that there are people in your life that need a hand up to help make life fair again.

Many people sit on the sidelines of life watching other people bring justice to a broken world. But that's not me, and I hope it's not you. As one person, you may not be able to change the whole world, but every day you have a chance to change the world of one person.

# CHAPTER TEN STUDY GUIDE

1. In what ways has life been unfair to you?


2. On the other hand, in what ways has life given you an unfair advantage?


3. Why do you think we are so aware of our own fair treatment, and yet, so unaware of the fair treatment of others?


4. When you think about fairness, do you immediately think about yourself? Write the names of at least two people you know who have a less fair life than you.


5. What is one way you could bring fairness or to someone at your school?


6. What could you do to play a role in international justice? How could you help with poverty, nourishment, and real life needs around the globe?

# 11

## CHAPTER ELEVEN

## CITIZENSHIP

When I met Mr. Audia, he seemed like a regular school teacher. Sure, he was excited about teaching, and that made him stand out, but he didn't have that larger-than-life persona where it makes you think the person is going to do something crazy. It came as a surprise, then, when I discovered what he had been up to.

Mr. Audia teaches at Cherry Creek School in Lowell, Michigan. When I started seeing articles in the paper about his class, I became very curious about the project they were doing. The next time I visited the school I walked in to see – hanging from the ceiling throughout the school – plastic bottles full of the nastiest, brownest drinking water I've ever seen. They were all over the place. When I asked Mr. Audia about it, he gave all the credit to the kids. "They're raising awareness for kids in

Haiti who don't have access to clean drinking water, and they're turning it into a full blown fundraiser," he said.

At the beginning of the year, Mr. Audia had given a short lesson on Haiti and how many of the people there lacked access to clean drinking water. He went through the statistics of how many people die each year, how many are malnourished, and how many had absolutely no access to safe drinking water. But then Mr. Audia did something else. He made it personal. Instead of simply talking about big numbers of people from a land "far far away," he began telling personal stories of kids who were the same age as the kids in his class. He made the connection. Every kid in class knew – *that could be me.*

In that moment the students in Mr. Audia's class took hold of a timeless truth that many adults fail to see: that we are all citizens of the same world, and that all lives have value.

Under this definition, citizenship is expanded to include more than the United States. More than the red, white, and blue. Under this definition, patriotism and loyalty to our country still rings true, but it does so with optimism and generosity toward the rest of the world.

The emerging generation will simply accept this as true.

This is why the kids in Mr. Audia's class turned their passion into a purpose. In a small rural town in Michigan, during an economic recession, a class of 25 kids raised over $2,000 to buy water filters for kids in Haiti. Absolutely astonishing.

○ ○ ○

As citizens of the world, we have a duty to take good care of what is entrusted to us. That means we have a lot of responsibility.

As a United States Citizen, you have many rights. You have the right to vote, the right to free speech, even the right to remain silent (haha). And with these rights come responsibilities. You have the right to earn an unlimited income with no salary caps (unlike communist China, for example), but with that right comes the responsibility to pay taxes. The more you make, the more you pay. Decide to skip that responsibility for too long, and you may really have to exercise your right to remain silent, as you are hauled off to the slammer.

The beauty of the whole democratic system is that you have a voice. You have an opportunity to be heard. This is why we have public elections. We get to choose who spends our tax money, and I want to have a say in who spends my money. Yet sadly, the population sector with the lowest voter turnout has always been young people ages 18 to 25.

Ironic, isn't it? The people who have just been given new rights (the right to vote), become disinterested and decide not to exercise that right for many years. Yet people in other countries around the world risk civil war, economic collapse, even their lives to earn this basic right.

As U.S. Citizens, it is our duty to exercise our rights and participate in the greatness of our democracy. As citizens of the world, it is our responsibility to find effective ways to bring justice and opportunity to the poor, the malnourished, and the hopeless.

If you are born in America, you are born into a system of wealth. You may not feel rich, but to the majority of the world, you are. But feeling guilty about your privileges does nothing to solve the problem. The problem is solved with action.

You are only one person. I am only one person. What can one citizen of the world do to "change the world?"

Your generation is already discovering new ways of living that lift people out of poverty. Microfinance provides a new way for everyday people to provide small business loans, as low as $20, to individuals who want to start businesses around the world. Buying fair trade coffee ensures the coffee farmer a fair price for his crop. Purchasing sweat-shop-free clothing is a way of reducing child labor and unfair working conditions overseas. And the ideas keep developing.

As a citizen of both the United States and of the world, your job is to take responsibility for your rights and then use those rights to provide resources and opportunities to our brothers and sisters who need it the most.

# CHAPTER ELEVEN STUDY GUIDE

1. Rate yourself on a scale of one to ten, with ten being the best. How are you doing with citizenship and the responsibility of your rights?

2. As a citizen of the United States, do you think your vote will make a difference? Why or why not?

3. As a citizen of the world, how do your daily actions affect the lives of other people around the globe?

4. Why do you think the kids in Mr. Audia's class were moved to action?

5. What is one specific way you can spend your money to help reduce global poverty?

# CHAPTER TWELVE

# A BIGGER STORY

Have you ever been with a group of people that are constantly retelling the same old jokes from back in the day? What about people who cannot stop talking about their future. They are going to be so great when they ...fill in the blank. Sometimes I just want to wave my hand in front of their faces and say, "What about the here and now?!!?" It's like they're stuck living in The Land of Once. Half of them live in Southern Once, and the other half live in Northern Once. The southerners say things like, *"Once, when I was captain of the high school football team, I led us to a state championship!"* The northerners, on the other hand, have a totally different accent. Theirs is more like, *"Once I get that new job, things will be so much better!"* And if you hang with either crowd for too long, you start to believe that your best days are either way behind you or way ahead of you.

I remember when I was about twelve I wanted nothing more in the world than to be a teenager. From what I heard, this would be the best time of my life. My Dad and I were working in our Christmas tree field one afternoon, and we paused to take a breather. I was daydreaming about becoming a teen and driving and having a girlfriend and all of that, when I asked my Dad what was the greatest time in his life. I was thinking he would say when he was sixteen, or perhaps when he was eighteen. I was really just looking for confirmation that the teen years were the best. So I asked him straight out.

He paused for a second, leaned into his shovel, and said with certainty,

## "...PROBABLY RIGHT NOW."

The way he said it was so riveting, so resolute, that I knew he meant it. If you could have heard his voice, there was no "probably" about it. And in those few words, my Dad imparted a worldview that sticks with me to this day. I remember these words when the weight of the world is pulling me to the south or to the north. And it's in these moments that I stop. I breathe. And I whisper to myself, "...Probably right now."

○ ○ ○

You have heard people say that life is a stage, and each one of us is the star in our own play about us. This almost seems true because when you think about it, for pete's sake, you are in every scene! Everywhere you go, there you are. You must be the star, right?

The trouble with this philosophy is that it leads to a *self*-centered, *self*-focused, *self*-ish life. You get a thrill when your life is going good, but when your plans fall apart (as all peoples' plans do from time to time) your life falls apart.

## WHEN LIFE IS ALL ABOUT YOUR STORY, IT ENDS UP BEING A VERY SMALL STORY INDEED.

Leaders are not like this. Leaders take life as a gift. They see each day as a new opportunity to play a part in a greater story. A story bigger than self... that is a grand concept. So how do you go from being a person who doesn't care to someone who really cares?

Answer: by putting others first. What do I mean by that? Do I mean putting the needs of others ahead of your own needs? Do I mean giving up the best piece of fried chicken, so your little sister can have the drumstick? Do I mean letting other people go first in line? Do I mean giving up your precious iPad time to spend time with grand-mama? Yes, I mean all of these things.

Caring is cultivated by small choices made over a lifetime, but taking that initial step (to care for others more than yourself) can seem counterintuitive to our human nature. *What about me? Who's looking out for me?* Don't feel bad, that question is common to humanity. It's part of our default settings.

I never had to teach my kids to say "mine!" I never sat them down and said, "Listen, here's what I want you to do: I want you to cry whenever you're hungry or poopy." No one has to teach these things because we are naturally focused on getting our own needs met.

But as we grow older, learning to recognize and meet the needs of others becomes the key ingredient to maturity. Becoming others-focused is the essential ingredient to becoming who you were meant to be. In his book, Blue Like Jazz[15], Donald Miller calls it "discovering that other people exist." This act of caring for others is what makes us fully human. It's what separates us from the animals.

**Side Note:** This is a great line to use on your best friend Bob. Next time Bob does something awkward at the lunch table (it could be anything, doesn't matter), just remark, "Bob! Come on! That's the one thing the separates us from the animals!" Bob will love this, I assure you.

Back to caring. Leaders choose to care even when we don't feel like it. I don't always feel like caring, but when I

[15] Miller, Donald. Blue like jazz. Nashville, Tenn.: Thomas Nelson; 2006.

force myself to do it, the feeling of satisfaction follows. If I wait for my emotions to lead the way, I will end up lying on the couch every night watching reruns of UFC while the world goes to you-know-where in a hand basket. So I kick myself in the butt and volunteer at the food bank, serve at the nonprofit organization, plan the neighborhood block party, and change my kids' diapers (and let me tell you as a father of twins, that is no small task).

## HERE'S THE TRUTH: LIFE IS FAR TOO GREAT TO LIVE IN SELFISHNESS.

If you spend your time living in The Land of Once, playing video games, checking your facebook a hundred times a day, and generally not caring about anyone else, you will ultimately end up shrinking from the greatest of who you are supposed to be – a person who cares, a person who serves a bigger story.

Like it or not, we are all subject to the natural law of sowing and reaping. When we sow seeds of kindness, when we invest deep into the soil of another person's soul, that's when we reap the harvest of a rich life.

So when should you start to care about living in this bigger world, this bigger story?

Probably right now.

# CHAPTER TWELVE STUDY GUIDE

1.  What influences do you have that are telling you life is "all about you?"

2.  Which do you think is easier: living for yourself or living for others? Which do you think is more noble, and why?

3.  Describe one person you know who lives for a purpose greater than themselves.

4.  If we went around and asked people at your school what you were all about, what would they say?

5.  Look into the future for a second. If someone who knows you had to summarize your entire life in two sentences or less, what would you want them to say?

## CHAPTER THIRTEEN

## A UNIFIED TEAM

So you're in an awkward group setting with a bunch of new people, and the leader starts out by saying, "Let's all go around the room and introduce ourselves, telling something interesting about ourselves." Or maybe the leader wants you to say something you're good at, or tell about your hobbies. This is called the "ice breaker." It's a game designed to put the group at ease and relieve the obvious tension in the room. The paradox is that the ice breaker actually starts out by achieving the opposite goal - it makes people feel more anxiety and more awkwardness, as they wait for their turn to speak.

So the room is quiet and awkward, and now it's even more awkward as people start giving their mini-speeches. Just remember that no one will remember what you're about to say... because they're too busy thinking about what they're going to say when it's their turn, and then they're analyzing what they just said when their turn is over. This isn't necessarily a good or a bad thing. It's just how we humans work.

You will notice that most people start out by taking their turn in as little time as possible. They just want to get the spotlight off them. This is like my wife: she doesn't like it when a group of people stares at her. And most people are this way. But the thing is, what the group really needs is for someone to stand up and pop the balloon, letting all the hot air and tension out of the room. Everyone is drowning in awkwardness until you do it, so you take it upon yourself to serve the group in this way.

It will be best to sit about halfway around the circle, right across from the group leader, so that your turn comes in the middle, when the tension is at its highest. You're not looking to get attention - you just want to help the group by, well... by breaking the ice of the ice breaker.

## HERE ARE MY TOP FIVE WAYS TO "BREAK THE ICE' OF THE ICE BREAKER:

1. Say, "I'm Tom Thelen, and I do Imagination Magic. I tell people to close their eyes and imagine that I have a piece of rope. Then imagine me cutting the rope in two. Now imagine that I just put the rope back together into one solid piece. Viola! Open your eyes!... Imagination Magic!" (Don't actually have the

group close their eyes; just describe to them how you do your Imagination Magic. This is key.)

2.  Introduce yourself as the person sitting next to you - the person whose turn is coming right after yours. Then act embarrassed, like you didn't mean to say that. (Note: this only works if you already know the name of the person sitting next to you.)

3.  Say, "I'm Tom Thelen, and one thing I'm good at is paint stirring. If someone has a can of paint that needs stirring, I'm all over it. I've been doing this since I was a small child, and I have become highly skilled in this regard."

4.  Say, "I'm Tom Thelen, and one thing people don't know about me is that I have only four toes on my left foot ... Motorcycle accident. It's really hard for me to talk about." If people ask to see the foot, just run out of the room screaming like you're having a flashback.

5.  Don't say anything at all. Instead, just shoot small fireworks out of your hat. (Note: you will need to acquire a hat that shoots small fireworks.)

The point is: it's not good for a group of people to sit silently in a room feeling shy, anxious, and embarrassed. We need someone besides the "actual leader" to say, "I'm not willing to let that happen. Not on my watch." Then we need that person to make us laugh - even at their expense. We need people who are willing help the leader achieve her goals. All the leader really wants is for the group members to know that they're in a safe place and that everything is going to be fine. And the group members want to be assured of the same thing. So even while the group is laughing at you, you should understand that we're all silently grateful for your kind act of self-sacrifice and servanthood.

The truth is: you're actually hoping that some other brave soul will do this before you have to. Because you know that if the room is still full of hot air when the spotlight finally gets to you, you will be the one to pop the balloon. This is your calling...

# YOU'RE AN ICE BREAKER BABY.

○ ○ ○

The best leaders become experts at team dynamics. They feel the pulse of the group, and they intuitively know what is needed for the team to achieve success.

In the 1960s a 27-year old professor at Ohio State University wrote an article that forever changed how the world would view team dynamics[16]. His name was Bruce Tuckman, and he titled the article *Tuckman's Stages*.

Tuckman maintained that every group goes through four stages of development: *forming, storming, norming, and*

---

[16] Abudi, Gina. "The Five Stages of Project Team Development." The Project Management Hut. N.p., 8 May 2010. Web. <http://www.pmhut.com/the-five-stages-of-project-team-development>.

*performing,* and if a group could successfully navigate through the stages, they would be able to function and outperform other (dysfunctional) groups.

## FORMING

In the forming stage, the group is testing the waters and getting to know each other; it's like a first date. And as the team roles become official, the group solidifies and enters a sort of honeymoon phase. Like most honeymoons, this phase is very short lived, and everything goes great. There is a lot of good will amongst the team members. It's fun. People are excited to be there – excited about the possibilities of the group.

As the leader it is important for you to help the team define its purpose, vision, mission, and roles.

- **PURPOSE** is the belief behind **why** the team exists; it's why you want to do something. *(i.e.: The Chicago High School Conservation Club (CHSCC) believes that access to clean drinking water is a universal right.)*

- **VISION** is **what** the team wants to do in light of their purpose. *(i.e.: CHSCC exists to provide clean drinking water to orphanages in third world countries.)*

- **MISSION** is the plan for **how** the team will accomplish its vision. *(i.e.: CHSCC will raise $5,000* *this school year to fund clean water filtration systems for orphanages in South Africa.)*

- **ROLES** are the individual assignments and responsibilities of each team member. *(i.e.: Mike will be the Treasurer, Elise will coordinate the fundraisers, etc.)*

If your team can successfully define your purpose, vision, mission, and roles *while still in the forming* stage, then you're building a firm foundation. Clarity is key. Make sure you involve the team in the decision making process.

Leadership guru Stephen Covey is famous for saying *"There is no commitment without involvement."* In other words, you must involve your team in the decision making process if you want their full commitment and energy. You must hear all the ideas, and then as a team, make the best decision for moving forward. If you can move forward on group consensus and the natural momentum of the forming stage, you can develop the stamina to weather the "storm" of the next stage.

## STORMING

The storming stage cannot be avoided – every successful group goes through it, so do not be alarmed when your group starts to "storm." In this stage, the group members start competing for power and influence. They begin debating which ideas are best for moving forward. In the Chicago High School example, the group could easily start storming over how the team will define its mission. One teammate wants to raise money to buy the water filters, another thinks the whole team should plan an African missions trip, still another thinks they should send the money straight to a non-profit organization in Africa.

You can see how easily the group dynamics will change from *Kumbaya around the campfire* (forming stage) to *"My ideas are better than yours!!!"* (storming stage).

*Inside Tip:* Watch your blind spots. Sometimes group members have a "hidden agenda," meaning they have an unspoken goal they're trying to achieve through the group. Perhaps a group member has something to gain if the group takes a certain action. Maybe their hidden agenda is to get money or power or fame or whatever else. Just know that it will be very hard to build a unified team if someone is operating with a hidden agenda. Don't get paranoid, but be diligent and explain the importance of being real, honest, and up front with everything.

During this stage, stamina is key. Hang in there. Don't get emotionally involved in your ideas. Don't make them "your baby." When everyone gets possessive about their ideas and when they're not willing to let "their baby" die, the group often gives in to the person who talks the longest or the loudest. And obviously, long and loud are not great qualifications for leadership.

Again, hear everyone ideas, and let them go through some healthy conflict, but be very clear that the accomplishments of the group will always be more important than the individual plans and projects of the group members.

If you are an insecure leader, the team could implode or stay in the storming stage for a very...

Long.

Time.

## NORMING

If you can find ways to value the contribution of each member, the group can ease into the norming stage. Publically praise each member's accomplishments and ideas, even if the group will ultimately go in another direction. Don't be fake, but genuinely seek diverse opinions on the group's direction.

Insecure leaders build consensus by surrounding themselves with yes-men. They quickly arrive at the norming stage, only to find themselves surrounded by mediocrity. Yes-Men (men or women) agree with whatever the leader says. They are too self-conscious to have a difference of opinion, to offer another solution, or to present a different angle. So the group slogs through at the pace of their overloaded, control freak leader. You end up with a low performing, dysfunctional group.

Not so with you. You want to reach a legitimate norming stage the old fashioned way, so you work through your problems, you build consensus, and you stress the team's goals over individual pet projects.

Be proactive and encourage the group to get all their ideas out during the meetings (no meeting-after-the-meeting in the school hallway). Tell them you subscribe to the iron-sharpens-iron principle and you value good, healthy conflict. When conflict is handled with mutual respect, it can actually produce some of the best, most effective ideas.

## PERFORMING

As the group's expectations for their purpose, vision, mission, and roles become clear, you can gain momentum to move into the performing stage. In this stage the group becomes a well-oiled machine, but it's important to note: NOT EVERY TEAM MAKES IT THIS FAR. Many teams thrive in the norming stage and nothing motivates them on to the performing stage.

When this happens, there are normally two factors at play: *a lack of trust* or *a lack of vision*. If I don't trust you, I can't follow you. If I don't know the vision, I cannot follow it... there is nothing to follow.

So to achieve the holy grail of group development, the performing stage, you must build trust and pour vision back into your team! When trust is achieved and the vision is clear, the team's performance level has potential to go through the roof. Perhaps you discover a way to double your goal and raise $10,000 for Africa. Maybe

there is a way to _____
(fill in the blank). For every team, your "blank" will be
different because your purpose is different.

Remember: as the leader, you are the glass ceiling. You
set the expectation for acceptable behavior, the mood of
the group, what can be achieved, and so on. You are it.
Nobody is going to be it for you. You are it by default.

o o o

When you find healing from your bitterness, you are set
free to become fully yourself. Only then can you grow into
the leader you were meant to be.

When I went through the character intervention program
on the Burdick's Farm all those years ago, it set me free.
This became the biggest gift of my life.

I learned to forgive my Dad. I learned to forgive myself. I
learned that forgiveness is a way of life. And today, as a
husband, a father of four great kids, as a speaker, and as
an author, I pass the torch on to you.

It's the TEEN LEADERSHIP REVOLUTION.

# AND YOU ARE LEADING IT.

# CHAPTER THIRTEEN STUDY GUIDE

1. Why do you think so many leaders neglect the art of group dynamics?


2. Take a minute to diagnose your team. Are you forming, storming, norming, or performing? Why?


3. What steps can you take to elevate your team to the next level of success?


4. In no more than one sentence each, write out your:

- Purpose (the Why):


- Vision (the What):


- Mission (the How):


5. What is one habit you can start today, that will build your leadership and character over the next year? Now go make it happen. Don't wait for permission.

## CHAPTER FOURTEEN

## SECRETS OF SUCCESS

If you skipped right to this chapter, shame on you. Go sit in the corner and give yourself a timeout.

There is no shortcut to success! You can't microwave it, fast-forward it, or compact it. Success is achieved by sustained effort over time. With that said, teens always ask, *"What are your secrets to success?"* So I've compiled them into this brief chapter. If you want my full answers, please read the rest of the book!

## SECRET 1 - BE A LEARNER

Developing a love for learning is the key to sustained growth as a person. I get so tired of talking to people who have learned all they ever want to know about life! It is the ultimate turn off – people who already know it all. So be teachable, and learn from your mistakes. Even better, find a mentor, and learn from the mistakes of others!

As a teen, this was the Burdick family for me. They had learned to weather the storms of life, so they taught me to do the same. I discovered how to turn my pain into a purpose, and it forever changed my life.

About two years ago, I went out of my way to ask an older man to be my mentor. He agreed, but only on one condition: that I be the one to determine when his advice is valuable and when it does not apply to my situation. Now that is wisdom: being secure enough to know you don't have all the answers.

The biggest way I learn today is through "boring stuff" like books, blogs, PBS, and NPR. Pretty glamorous, I know. And then I go to bed early with a nice warm glass of milk. But seriously, I consume valuable resources, I develop healthy relationships, and I tune out the static that clutters my life. I love to learn, and I desire wisdom!

# SECRET 2 - BE AN OWNER

I am the only person responsible for my life, my actions, my successes, and my failures. Outside forces and life circumstances come and go, so I resist the urge to blame anything on the actions of others or on situations that are out of my control. I own my life. I own my results.

As an owner, I accept that no one is going to do it for me. No one is going to give me permission, hand it to me on a silver platter, or give me the opportunity of my dreams. So I don't wait for opportunities – I create them. I weigh the risks, then I take action knowing that nothing of value comes without great sacrifice.

As an owner, I choose to step up to the plate of life knowing that every failure can bring me one step closer to success. I refuse to be a spectator, to wait around on-deck, or to stand in the batter's box waiting for the perfect pitch. I am not luckier than the rest, and I don't have the highest batting average, but simply because I take more swings, I create more success.

# SECRET 3 - BE THE CHANGE

Ghandi said to *be the change you want to see in the world*. It's very easy to make commentary on why things should be better and why everyone else is doing it wrong, but it's another thing entirely to just make it better.

Being the change means making the same decisions in private as you do in public. It means being a person of character and choosing the to do right even when it is inconvenient. It means realizing how small decisions have a profound effect on yourself, your family, and on your neighbors across the street and around the world. No one else is going to do it for you. **_YOU_ MUST BE THE CHANGE.**

# CHAPTER FOURTEEN STUDY GUIDE

1. What types of influences can communicate that success comes quick and easy?

2. Describe what it is like to talk with someone who doesn't love to learn?

3. Name three influences or resources you can use to develop yourself as a person.

4. Why do you think it is so easy to blame your life circumstances on others?

5. Why do you hesitate to take more "at-bats" or more swings in life? What one thing is holding you back?

6. How can you **be the change** you want to see in your school? In your family? Write your plan below:

# MAKE IT HAPPEN!

*Think you've got what it takes to be a part of the*
*TEEN LEADERSHIP REVOLUTION?*

Join us online at http://TeenLeadershipRevolution.com
and receive the following free stuff:

- Video message from me, Tom Thelen

- Free subscription to the newsletter

- Free printable copy of the TLR Manifesto

- Free TLR 5-STEP GROWTH ACTION PLAN

- Free printable Event Planning Guide

- Free downloadable Desktops & Posters

More than anything, I want you to succeed by setting
other students free and helping them live a bigger story,
and that's why I'm making all of these resources available
to you free of charge. The only thing we're missing now...

# ...IS YOU.

Join for free at http://TeenLeadershipRevolution.com

# TEEN
## LEADERSHIP
## REVOLUTION
# MANIFESTO

1. We **RISE ABOVE** bitterness, negativity, and addiction.
2. We **DREAM BIGGER DREAMS**, serving a purpose greater than ourselves.
3. We turn our **PAIN INTO A PURPOSE**, uncovering *why* we must lead.
4. We turn our **PURPOSE INTO A VISION**, discovering *what* we must do.
5. We turn our **VISION INTO A MISSION**, discovering *how* we're going to do it.
6. We **BUILD CHARACTER** through self-discipline and courage.
7. We are the **FIRST FOLLOWERS** of great books, mentors, and leaders.
8. We are **TEAM PLAYERS**, putting the needs of others ahead of ourselves.
9. We are **GRATEFUL** for each day – the gift of starting fresh.
10. We **GO FURTHER** than anyone expects us to, including ourselves.

**We are the TEEN LEADERSHIP REVOLUTION.**

Signed _____ Signed_____
(Tom Thelen)                      (              )

## ABOUT THE AUTHOR:

Tom Thelen, author of *Teen Leadership Revolution*, is a youth speaker whose message on teen leadership and bullying prevention has reached over 500 youth audiences since 2002. He speaks at youth conferences and school assemblies teaching students to turn their pain around for a positive purpose. Tom has been featured on PBS, The National Association of Student Councils, YMCA Leadership Summits, and The National Honor Society.

As a youth speaker, Tom gives students practical strategies for taking responsibility and developing rock solid character. His message takes students on a journey through his own life story including a character intervention counseling program he experienced as a teen and how he learned to use self-discipline to overcome great adversity. He goes on to describe real-life success stories of today's students who are making a difference. Tom is a gifted motivator who relates to teens with stories that touch the heart and make them laugh. His high-energy school assembly programs provide an experience students never forget. Tom lives in Michigan with his wife Casie and their four children.

**CONNECT WITH TOM:**

Web: TomThelen.com

Email: Tom@TomThelen.com

**BOOK TOM FOR A SCHOOL ASSEMBLY OR CONFERENCE:**

Tami Wernette, Character Programs

(616) 987-0444 | Tami@CharacterPrograms.Org